The Gospel of
MichelAngelo Buonarroti

The Gospel of
MichelAngelo Buonarroti

D.A. Vid

iUniverse

THE GOSPEL OF MICHELANGELO BUONARROTI

Scripture quotations marked JB are from The Jerusalem Bible, copyright © 1966 by Darton, Longman & Todd, Ltd. and Doubleday, a division of Bantam Doubleday Dell Publishing Group, Inc. Reprinted by permission.

iUniverse books may be ordered through booksellers or by contacting:

iUniverse
1663 Liberty Drive
Bloomington, IN 47403
www.iuniverse.com
1-800-Authors (1-800-288-4677)

ISBN: 978-1-6632-0280-2 (sc)
ISBN: 978-1-6632-0287-1 (e)

Print information available on the last page.

iUniverse rev. date: 06/16/2020

Contents

All but Preface Poems and Surfing Eckhart first appeared in SLOVO/WORD, a Russian/English Journal.

Fragment also appeared in Last Judgment (iUniverse 2014).

For Johanna and Yevgeniy Sokolovskiy

David, I carefully read and reread the poems you sent me. They absolutely stun by their intellectual grandeur. Also what strikes me as truly remarkable is their extremely condensed (concise?) language. I think you put in one line more than what the majority of poets put in one stanza. Your poems are so emotionally and intellectually charged that I wonder whether it is feasible to transcend what you do using English language (at least in its present condition). When T.S. Eliot published his "Prufrock and Other Observations" in 1917, one literary critic said that the poet "reinvented English poetry." I think that your poetry is so powerful and original that you deserve the same comment.

Yevgeniy Sokolovskiy

Preface

SYLPH

Tara

Tara fashioned the face at 17. To speak the artist in her **soul.** She's
Only *gamed* at lovely. Pontificate is ugly. She's '*such,*' that much. *All*

Godly spoken. Heart breaks all broken. Mends **all** whole. Coil wanes
To **faintly** dervish. All least must perish. All famished rarish. **All** *envy*

Even. And **brag** somehow to leaven. The wound were maven. All
Healed by cloven. Death kisses life. And touch is driven. The imp

Is schooled in given. Can paint or feint, drive straw to spa, cold *sin*
To garish. This wench upends wielded decay just when all night *has*

Sway and dark is poised to scatter. Even *the bite* yields better. Warm
Chills all health. Stealth fills. Wealth beckons. Odd reckons. Sleep

Chances wake for pity's sake as might all Baptist, prophet. **No** *rank*
Messiah'd tough it. Rude splits infinitive. Itch laves. Our Tara *saves!*

J.E.Swartz 1982

MAGNIFICAT FIVE

M. Hassan

Magnificat? This *Vid* is caught. Even the bend of elbow churns
My spirit. This child of my own **child** chains all addiction, heals

My heart. There, she of wave's texture dares turn to gaze at one
Old man. By such ***Creation*** turns! Am cast adrift or cast at last

In stone. An instant of her breath is boundless Being. Aside or
Simply seeing—a glance, an imprint, grace, devotion. To dare to

Flick a page? The notion! She swims upon my soul. And held to
Task, for simply such I spoil. A lake of tears bemoans her past.

That past might last? All coming dust? All eyes must weep, for
Nations sleep, and lust is trust. Suffer her not to peek! Suffer

Her *not* to wither. May glance restore *all* Eden with her. Let all
Odd future *perish*. 'Tis *now* I cherish. Magnificat? A *Vid* a Gott.

MONS VENERIS

S. M. S. J. M. 2019

Wounded cleft suckles a mate at his 60ᵗʰ?
Can natal curiosity recover a tremulous youth?
Or simply a tree upended by a storm?

FRAGMENT: a prayer

Help me, dearest Lord Jehovah, sense you
    Even cramped in the wounded sky;
    Persuade me of your imprint in necrotic by and by?
The bundled rag-flesh in your teeming inviolable ovens;
    Aid all compassion for the spikes in our crucified Cousins.
Help me to feast
On
    Kikes and covens.

]]

Give me to sense your presence in the severed limb;
    Clarify a whisper of the stunted kin
Leaking saliva, misshapen lips;
    Inscrutable numinous welter of ALL soupy drips,
    Sanctify each torment of your awesome glottis;
    Ready my acceptance of the CANT that caught us,
    ALL titillation, torture;
Help me to feed your furnace, nurture—
    Dentures of departed genius,
    Pustules and decay;
YOUR MIGHTY SWAY—
    Demean us.
    Govern and renew each syllable, corporeal
Despair,
    Ease me into your fetid care,
    Settle my wayward tissues,
    Pacify with partial, even utter,
    Each sacrifice,
    Spermatorrhea, udder.

    Waken me glad and newlywed, my blighted birth, the earth, the dread, ALL
    Treacle, all malformed.
    Engender in me warm,

A heart for tart despair, for hurt-the-curts, for prayer,
  For all that languish in our sullen air,
  For cancroid blossoms,

  For ALL the awesomes—
  For deficit of pity,
  Children choked or swollen in the ravished cities,

Enable all Cain (or sacrificed Abels?), to paucity of lamb on a billion tables.
  Sleep soundly in defeat
  With minimal deceit
  And hand in buttered sand to eat.
  And let ALL wonderment repeat for 30 million years,
  For queers & seers,
  Still-born, the torn, ridiculed, deceased,
  And all the rosaries they've squeezed
  Their prophets seized—in stasis or in motion.

]]

  The crapped, or trapped in LATEST lotion—all bounty such,
  Such notion;
  Grant unto us, dear God, a space of saving grace, a taste, a trace, of face,
  A proper brace—
  & limitless devotion.

                                                    December 30, 2010

The Gospel of Buonarroti Canto one

"Help me, dearest Lord Jehovah, sense you
Even cramped in the wounded sky."

D.A. Vid

BC [the chapel ceiling]

One   Jonah
Three   Serpent
Five   Jeremiah
Seven   Light from Darkness
Nine   Earth from Waters

AD [his choice]

Two   Demonic swine
Four   Magi
Six   Fig tree
Eight   Baptist
Ten   Levitation

ONE

Yahweh had arranged that a great fish should be there to swallow Jonah; and Jonah remained in the belly of the fish for three days and three nights. From the belly of the fish he prayed to Yahweh, his God. . . . . Yahweh spoke to the fish, which then vomited Jonah on to the shore.

Jonah 2:1-11

> Jonah, astounding, metaphysician, held us in a convoluted **spiral**
> Shredding the absolute black. Even in his mute *palpations,* trapped
>
> In the belly of a fish, somehow forecast the undulations of some
> Dizzy sextillion suns, a whorl of naked fire, a kiss a **searing** scar.
>
> It seems or seemed just then in viscous void what fearful bounty
> *Shivered,* quaked at what we were or were to be, Jehovah's *fractious*
>
> Progeny, from glutinous foment's slime past Upward GAINING
> SPINE**,** Mankind and what gave bread and *wine to each* **demonic**
>
> Chthonic essence—*stark, diffuse* in time. Yet Jonah? What comely
> **Calves** are these? What glossy limpid limbs, confection? **Some**
>
> Suchness of his feel? What brainless zeal, what squeal? 'D wreak
> A boundless vengeance on the quiet? Or scab what *fruitless* riot?

TWO

They stood there shouting, "What do you want with us, Son of God? Have you come here to torture us before the time? . . . If you cast us out, send us into the herd of pigs." And he said to them, "Go then," and they came out and made for the pigs; and at that the whole herd charged down the cliff into the lake and perished. . . .

Matthew 9:29-33

> *Shimmer* in the quiet sky, pale bleed of blue, some *15 hundred* lilac
> Swine, *their grease and* sweat, stink-ravaged sun and rapt ingestion.
>
> There just there a Christ inclines voiceless in the suck & roar, to
> Heal and bring to heel pigs and devils. Demonic *shrieks* erupt a
>
> Boundless eructation, the fright sensation, the feel, *odd squeal* as
> *Beasts* turn tail and charge the cliff, snort rattle quake, a bleating
>
> Fury, that Hell itself *would shudder, worry that fevered* lard *cascading*
> Into SMACK! Just there just then a Demon-Gott's attack, from
>
> Outer, inner, poised, *brute* carnage pig upon the stacks **viscera**
> Impinging on abyss, small **matter snout** their snout has kissed,
>
> Obscenity of ragged carnal in the motion, surge. Are moments
> Into *IT:* the Christly Mensch has quelled a TORRID horrid fit.

THREE

So Moses fashioned a bronze serpent which he put on a standard, and if anyone
was bitten by a serpent, he looked at the bronze serpent and lived.

Numbers 21:9

> A serpent coils the vertical, but bronze, a sign, a standard &
> No threat—just to its left the **faithless** in **their** boil, curse,
>
> Shriek, **their** quest. Where is this snake in God's **immortal**
> **Kingdom?** How prefigure Son upon a Cross? Of **very self**
>
> The saved gaze on in quiet; guilty riot, sheer legacy a **spasm**
> Of pain unending—'tis such **Jehovah's** bending, such those

Leaks no viper'd heal: for retribution judicates fierce rending
Of the Soul! They **writhe** upon the soil, and **no** amount of

Beauty in their straits redeems obscene, no jutting flank, no
Finery, nor comely garment eases, while **right** the righteous

Gesture, precurse their truest Son. This been was Him? Or
Cruciform salvation is the norm? & corpus warm. To **term!**

FOUR

Having listened to what the king had to say, they set out. And there in front of
them was the star they saw rising; it went forward and halted over the place where
the child was. The sight of the star filled them with delight, and going into the
house they saw the child with his mother Mary, and falling to their knees they did
him homage. Then, opening their treasures, they offered him gifts of gold and
frankincense and myrrh.

Matthew 2:9-12

We **found** a savior in a shed suffused by soft **supernal** light, the
Gentle 3 God humbled and as **much** ourselves, struck dumb; so

Thankful for the sight, our presents seemed *utterly unequal* to the
Child, and **3 together** Godlike beings, whose **simple** garments

Gleamed one *Godly* glow which tore at eyes and sucked *our inner*
Strength. What **were** these? And how adorn with frankincense?

Frail gold and *myrrh,* all lavish gifts brought *humble* by the vision.
WHICH was this child, and, **further, was** its mother? The man

Seemed curiously unmoved, possessor of a studied calm, aloof
From precious gift or balm, content at most to carry on his infant

Son's odd numinously mission. ALL knew from years to come
We'd treasure **this huge mystery** captive mercy in our **hearts.**

FIVE

"When you tell this people all these words and they ask you, 'Why has Yahweh decreed this appalling disaster for us? What is our crime? What sin have we committed against Yahweh our God?' then you are to answer, 'It is because your ancestors abandoned me—it is Yahweh who speaks—and followed alien gods, and served and worshipped them. They abandoned me and did not keep my Law.'"

Jeremiah 16:10-11

Jeremiah **grims** his eloquent hand, devours an outward **message**
While the left pours pain toward leather leggings. Eloquent the bulk

Of *his existence.* Most soul would trade salvation for a squint a hint,
Of *this old man,* this bitter prophet. *Cold brain* is **twined** with **fury.**

Summons in fact despair that skewed Creation, ceased ignores a feast.
Messiahs come? And gone? Where can he suffer fools enough to

Gather some **scant** few to fruitful living? Our mild Yahweh *strives*
By this old man's account, forgiving. Yet even celestial patience's

Tried. The best incline toward slumber, odd gambol in the rack of
Pain, *scorn Gott as* void, recoil, *revoke, stark* genius, hug, **a** glitter of

Disdain. Angel of Hell itself, see not **this** master's *inward, wizened*
Homely? That Future's black? That void's a lack and grim is lonely!

SIX

As he was returning to the city in the early morning, he felt hungry. Seeing a fig tree by the road, he went up to it and found nothing on it but leaves. And he said to it, "May you never bear fruit again"; and at that instant the fig tree withered.

Matthew 21:18-20

A tree which bears no fruit cannot **deserve** to live? **Such** is the
Impulse of a being whose script is patently *"Forgive"*? Or canon

Is to mystify God's Law, whose touch *would grace* both Herod's
Wench and Baptist's countenance on a platter, Herod *himself or*

Helpmate's *daughter?* Odd anger, misogyny or *slaughter? "Here IS*
My judgment, rest in pain, I'd have my fig; 'tis JUST, **that** *plain. Who*

Therefore scants shall claim at last what bounty lacks; this curse securely
On its back, 'tis my attack . . . Just WITHER!" "Whither? Whether?

Our cripples dance, a cancer's given? By chance forgiven?" "I'd query,
Query weary, Iscariot who chose for most 'Miscarry it.' Choose to sleep

The day God *pruned our weeds. Choose the deeds. Moses gave Ten, we*
Lack Eleven. *Judas the Maven? Barren afraid, betrayed of Heaven."*

SEVEN

God said, "Let there be light," and there was light. God saw that light was good, and God divided light from darkness. God called light "day," and darkness he called "night." Evening came and morning came: the first day.

D.A. Vid

Genesis 1:3-5

A **whirling** ungodly Gott! Would **rip** the emerald sky from black,
Shred wind from stars, wrest sun from bleeding pitch, embark on

Wildest even in His manic mind? endeavor. Dear Christ, who was
To be, what **fever!** There the **boundless** empyrean **waste,** there

Sudden be violated into being, there the chastened chased! What
Rage endured Creator toward *such* wisdom! How huge this thrust

To CONCEPT! A deity looms large, **wrenching** the **vast abyss;**
We watch from fragile vantage point His motions. *Eye gownèd belly*

Of Creator, eye monster rather, madness rapt erupting into forms,
A whole whose birth none could foresee. And loneliness enough?

To thrust such terror, rage to be? How celebrate this violation of
Of His blood that skewed a doomed eternal ripple on the quiet?

EIGHT

Then Jesus appeared: he came from Galilee to the Jordan to be baptized by John. John tried to dissuade him. "It is I who need baptism from you" he said "and yet you come to me!" But Jesus replied, "Leave it like this for the time being; it is fitting that we should, in this way, do all that righteousness demands." At this John gave in to him.

As soon as Jesus was baptized he came up from the water, and suddenly the heavens opened and he saw the Spirit of God descending like a dove and coming down on him.

Matthew 3:12-16

The **Baptist** is **a fearful Sight,** from **matted** crown to jagged fright,
A countenance full scabbed and scarred; **the beard** spits notions of

8

Dull twine and shard. As if **he gathered** Hell to guard with **insect,**
Purple weed, that plain, a hand unkempt with hair and stain, intent,

His garments *properly* attack, *a moth* assault on *simply black, or coarsely*
Cousin gathered sack, against broad bone and wiry frame, excess of

Height that fells the tame, *or injured* lame who cower under. But lad
He grips NO manner ordure, **some 30** years, sleek but soft, WITH

Bearing princely and of regal loft, full cleanly, Noble, with a glance
That shears, to scar or heal ill matter years OR shrugs a lesser wit &

Strength, to drain from fury, pith and length, the Baptist's grasp—
All in true query of an *aged lad,* a greater rout, what doubt he had.

NINE

God said, "Let there be a vault in the waters to divide the waters in two." And so it
was. God made the vault, and it divided the waters above the vault from the waters
under the vault. God called the vault "heaven.". . . . God said, "Let the waters under
heaven come together into a single mass, and let dry land appear."

Genesis 1:6-10

God the **Father explodes** from the brawn of Gott! Cerebral flash
Is what He's caught, surge *to wrestle water's* utter into Being. Simply

Confront just how He spirals through the Heavens. And *there his*
Puta! A human-blind Creator summons at the summit, a guttural

Bending *burst of sound.* Ach hear Him proudly rev *immortal engines.*
HE is Creator. HE is without limit! HE shall have His way! *Such*

Awesome navigation wrests odd night from Day, all substance from
Primordial soup, wrests trilobite, nucleus, e'en **atom.** In time **His**

Adam, for *nothing* can hinder boundless thirst, exuberance, all riot,
Blunder, texture, tortured fabric of the quiet. Universe **itself** SO

Riven! God bursts from Gott! This ordered **ardor** rips at servant
Satan. *Curse him?* Almighty torsion? Laceration? lesion of His lap.

TEN

In the fourth watch of the night he went towards them, walking on the lake, and
when the disciples saw him . . . they were terrified. . . . Jesus called out to them,
saying, "Courage! It is I! Do not be afraid." It was Peter who answered, "Lord," he
said "if it is you let me come to you across the water." "Come," said Jesus. Then
Peter got out of the boat and started walking toward Jesus across the water. . . .

Matthew 14:26-30

The mountain where last we looked was bathed in evening light. But
Storm was here, head-wind and angry clouds that buffeted our skiff,

Fear in itself but not so fearful as that figure on the turbulent waters.
The ghost it seemed of very Christ retired to take a solace to himself

Upon the peak, while kindred souls here rested from their oars; and
Lingering fragments of the mob, the half *He'd* healed. *But then, quite*

Then a solitary guest, a **specter** against the reddened sky, remote **yet**
Nearing. *"Who's there?"* Cried **John?** Cried Matthew, **Peter,** Mark?

"Who's there?"— WHO mattered less than fury collective as sea itself
Churned *dread* itself to complement our haste. *And* thing-like thing

Responded: "Christ!" Peter himself: "Then let me walk to thee!" Then Son:
"Come." "Ach Gott, I sink!" A Son of God eased both Men to the skiff.

2014-17

The Gospel of Buonarroti
Canto two

If you've read something better,
Chances are I wrote it.

D.A. Vid

BC {the chapel ceiling]

Eleven	Plants Sun Moon
Thirteen	Daniel
Fifteen	Haman
Seventeen	Ezekiel
Nineteen	Adam

AD [his choice]

Twelve	Ezras
Fourteen	Lazarus
Sixteen	Toward Golgotha
Eighteen	Temple cleansing
Twenty	Transfiguration

11

ELEVEN

God said, "Let the earth produce vegetation. . . . . . . Let there be lights in the vault of heaven to divide day from night.". . . . . God made the two great lights: the greater light to govern the day, the smaller light to govern the night, and the stars.

Genesis 1:11-17

> What quakes this glint of sun and moon? What whirl in trenchant
> Weary strength, gives rise to Dawn, gives flank, gives brawn, OR
>
> Gentle transition, plant and tree, what calmer God now carefully
> Seeds what be. The lilt is HE? a careful abiding Christ: that lame
>
> Can walk and blind can see. [Creator seeds **this** soil **so** tenderly?]
> What glimpse of bird and brush is still to come? What summons
>
> Culls dull dirt to mellow plum? **To** apple [good] **all** growth [that
> Could], the vine that twined, or spruce or kined? a host of green,
>
> *From nuance*, fill, the lilac, rose, the willow weeping *still,* but not
> From ill intention, use, a simple truth to path abstruse, for *calmer*
>
> God *endured* the *sweetest* length, a means *perhaps*, an asp for *strength.*
> Though habits hasten Adam's lapse, the isn't future, *even* **torture.**

TWELVE

Herod was furious when he realized that he had been outwitted by the wise men, and in Bethlehem and its surrounding district he had all the male children killed who were two years old or under, reckoning by the date he had been careful to ask the wise men.

13

Matthew 2:16-17

> *"What* child *is this? A male?"* In the low clay *room no s*oldier is
> Erect, even who bears a **sack of** heads that trails a crimson
>
> On the clay tile floor. *"The youth? Ezra." "And a certain male?*
> *His age?"* They cluster at a fire. "36 months; *is certain."* "You
>
> *The mother?" "And Benzion you the father?" "How old man is this*
> *Lad? Speak truly." "Elsbeth* can vouch for him. 'Tis clear she
>
> *Says a truth! 3 years." "Such fabrication! Punishment? Simple. Strip*
> *His garment."* Suddenly even the captive *males* are weeping. 3
>
> Guards nudge forth to bare *the lad.* All sob. *"Here, kneel. The*
> *Pain is quick."* In arc from high *(the smoke hole), sword* cleaves
>
> Now nameless head from *shoulders* to splatter on the clay tile
> Floor. In a welt of crimson glitters the token *silver medallion.*

THIRTEEN

The king conferred high rank on Daniel and gave him many handsome presents. He also made him governor of the whole province of Babylon and head of all the sages of Babylon. At Daniel's request, however, the king entrusted the affairs of the province of Babylon to Shadrach, Meshach and Abednego; Daniel himself remained at court.

Daniel 2:48-49

> Daniel, who braved the **Lion's** lust, who ground his fears to dust,
> Who scorned the pitch of Hell, proclaiming Son's emphatic birth.
>
> There muscle-laden Puta *hefts* the Book! To grimace *at its* weight?
> To hush, to wait, while Heaven coughs its phlegm, Satan in deed

Fit guardian of the **Gate,** were Mercy omnipresent, there **Jesu** at
His supper! *There* Jesu Christ, I suffer! There Shadrach, Meshach,

Abednego, who deviled Fire itself. Or Pope to disbelief: a wound
Of *summons* in the commons? A blast like no-man's? There Leaks

The pitch of itch, the pen! There seeks aloft the **cough** and grin!
Man's victory's pyrrhic, *starved or prim.* Daniel, sweet shadow licks

Your chin! Come, master, prophet, carve it thin! Your world SO
Narrow binds the Cosmos. So steady all poem to quest *for proses.*

FOURTEEN

Martha said to him, "Lord, by now he will smell; this is the fourth day." Jesus
replied, "Have I not told you that if you believe you will see the glory of God?"
So they took away the stone. Jesus . . . . cried in a loud voice, "Lazarus, here!
Come out!" The dead man came out, his feet and hands bound with bands of stuff
and a cloth round his face. Jesus said to them, "Unbind him, let him go free."

John 11:39-44

Each swore *the male* deceased, and hours so—such *stiffening* hardly
Reclined **upon the cot,** Lazarus alive? **The Master** intoned, *"He*

Sleeps." Ushered the *muttering* family out and us to guard the door.
"He sleeps?" slurred John, his voice *a certain tremor* in *a quie*t so thick

VOICE cut it like a knife. Again: *"Sleeps?" "Why not?" "Come now,*
Master, a truer **course is** *not to frighten us."* "Here, Peter, kiss his lips."

WAS said**!** I shudder yet. *"KISS THEM?" "Ach ja,* unruly *monk."*
"Dear sire, I shall not *keep my stomach." AND THEN* our Jesu knelt

> Where even cadaver smelled *and placed* His *lips* on *lips. "What make*
> *You there?"* The answer curt . . . *"Ach make a man!" "And* **kiss** *that*
>
> *Heap?" "He is! He is asleep!" Then, simply put, this* Lazarus *resumed*
> To color *even* quick. It *wrenched* my guts! [***But*** *cleared 10* **hundred!**]

FIFTEEN

When the king returned from the palace garden into the banqueting hall, he found Haman huddled across the couch where Esther was reclining. "What!" the king exclaimed. "Is he going to rape the queen before my eyes in my own palace?" The words were scarcely out of his mouth when a veil was thrown over Haman's face. Harbona, one of the eunuchs attending the queen, was present. "How convenient! There is that fifty-cubit gallows which Haman ran up for Mordecai, whose report saved the king's life. It is all ready at his house." "Hang him on it" said the king.

Esther 7:8-10

> Haman, who'd skewer Semite, pinned to a Leafless Tree. Who'd
> Nail his Esther to the boards and much the same on CALVARY.
>
> Viceroy to *Ahasuerus*, he lunges into Vision. See there the pathos
> Of his twisted corpus! Who'd burn the Jews in masse for an old
>
> Man's wicked slight, who'd spend his youth prefiguring the Cross.
> And where in Godly Kingdom is the loss? **Pure** Esther shapes a
>
> Murderous off-spring in the belly, seeks senile Kingship's *darkly*
> Retribution, this Haman **a neat** solution, and brings on PURIM
>
> For the wayward flock that some say brought God under. Such
> Story's Gospel blended with despair, a scent of *Germaine* ovens
>
> In the air, a comely plot. Some keep the tale on frontispiece, or
> Quiet. No manly Mystery this—the yarn *is* gapped. Hand riots!

16

SIXTEEN

On their way out, they came upon a man from Cyrene, Simon by name, and enlisted him to carry his cross.

Matthew 27:32-33

> You, I, we, ALL *saw Savior struggle* with that great rough wooden
> Cross toward Golgotha, *belly, back, visage* contorted with its heft.
>
> **Not yet** the sky was cleft, was **simply** toil on a dusty **path, and**
> *Thousands* looking on. The pain of us was such as mirror ache of
>
> Christ, there, just there alone, feet clutching dust and rock upon
> *Seldom traversed path* but for to perish. *This* mensch we cherished!
>
> Bloody countenance *ennobled* by the barbs of wreath with which
> They crowned Him. Fierce aching lunge laid low by that which
>
> **Pressed** Him into earth. THIS the child 3 *Magi* graced at birth,
> His mother somewhere weeping in the throng. *"Come,* move it,
>
> *Come, move on!"* To witness *goodness* humbled *such tormented,* **that**
> Even the Eleven were **eager** to let Him die. *"There, I'll take it."*

SEVENTEEN

[Yahweh] . . . said, "Go and shut yourself in your house. Son of man, bonds are now about to be laid on you; you will be bound with them and will not be able to mix with others. I am going to make your tongue stick to the roof of your mouth; you will be dumb; you will stop warning them, for they are a set of rebels. When I speak to you, I shall open your mouth and you will tell them, 'The Lord Yahweh says this.' Whoever will listen, let him listen; whoever will not, let him not; for they are a set of rebels."

Ezekiel 3:25-28

> Startled, Ezekiel quakes from work to address his God. The God
> Is hardly odd, so stern, *so unforgiving.* Would each and every burn
>
> Without repentance, shed *each false* gods to cringe for absolution?
> *What force is* there, what *Sin, ablution?* This old man's old, a proper
>
> Prophet, years etched upon his face. Puta, facing, fails to detect a
> Message. That SAGE must shudder. The message has no Mother.
>
> Ezekiel traces eternal worm. For worm has turn. No Torah more a
> Prescient, one cannot deny the Future. And Future torture? From
>
> *Presently deceased,* to ancients rotting, Judaic God alone is Godding,
> From thorns, pierced flesh, rude rood to itch and *"Moses chose us"*
>
> Baseless kitsch. One path remains *aspiring zealot* to endure; regard
> *The empty tomb of "Christ." In God* we trust? *Led* flock *to range there.*

EIGHTEEN

Jesus then went into the Temple and drove out all those who were selling and buying there; he upset the tables of the money changers and the chairs of those who were selling pigeons.

Matthew 21:12-13

> **Was it simply** outrage the Master stirred, that and not his Word?
> Some judge his voyage ended at the temple, cleansing the money
>
> *Changers and the* thieves, *such bartered* assorted pigeons, goods, this
> Prism prison of our Needs. Yahweh Himself a brave investment,

Inched toward glory, mortal **wealth the truer** story. With paper's
Exchange in sockets where injury was a debt and scab the healer,

Sure *manifest to dealer* at his table, where **Cain slew** dividend and
Worshipped able, paid tribute to his Tribune on a gilded tributary.

Whe*re poverty* was every to the poor in heart, who lacked all path
To start, forgone odd manner *of repentance*, the gaol a lighter sentence

Than the fire of debtor in his *Godly* jail; or gel or poison, a wad of
Current foison to swallow raw *or choke* the heart. Quaker bake or?

NINETEEN

Yahweh God fashioned man of dust from the soil. Then he breathed into his
nostrils a breath of life, and thus man became a living being.

Genesis 2:7

    His genitalia like petals against a thigh sweet Adam contained
    An arm extended, greets Gott above careening with Creation,

    This languid lad, a delicate selection, yields surge, feels spark,
    Spurns stasis. Just centimeters distant from that Godly touch,

    Kindled into life and basis. One wonders **if** it's God he faces?
    That thrust from brain pan, **celestial** Crew, **all hue** but blue,

    E'en Eve perhaps, or youthful Jesu, a coming life, a swarming
    Melody of Christ! From galaxy to planet waning's charged, *'tis*

    Good enlarged, and Yahweh clenched to let it out, *Spermatozoon*
    Of inception, first phase of humankind's *perception,* from Duty,

From Beauty poised in indolence, to Satan's prance, to dance.
Adam though leapt from dirt to seed to beauteous proportion.

TWENTY

Six days later, Jesus took with him Peter and James and his brother John and led them up a high mountain where they could be alone. There in their presence he was transfigured; his face shone like the sun and his clothes became as white as the light.

Matthew 17: 1-3

> Upon a high and *holy mountain* came a *vision struck* them dumb,
> Peter, *James* and John, for suddenly *was Christ in all* His *radiant*
>
> Glory. There, just there, had they assayed an **Indic Kief,** was
> Intensity; some thousand grams beyond belief *transfigured* soul
>
> They had often sought to touch, *a sudden such,* presence *million*
> Fold increased in just His garment, *blinding* **white,** a look that
>
> Seared them quite, a brazen gaze intruding on their soul. And
> Fell to grovel soil, to promise such glad devotion as 'D shield
>
> Them from his eyes: *"Ach God sweet God beatitude your sighs!"*
> The swirl of incandescence, for sun poured from His visage,
>
> *Then cloud* appeared, *eclipsing all but* Christ, a voice until *relented*
> Had *them* twice upon the earth, cowering in fear of retribution.

2014-17

The Gospel of Buonarroti
Canto three

"Help me, dearest Lord Jehovah, sense you
Even cramped in the wounded sky."

D.A. Vid

BC [the chapel ceiling]

Twenty-one   Eve
Twenty-three   The Fall
Twenty-five   Isaiah
Twenty-seven   Judith
Twenty-nine   Joel

AD [his choice]

Twenty-two   Resurrection
Twenty-four   Supper of thousands
Twenty-six   Annunciation
Twenty-eight   Gethsemane
Thirty   A paralytic

TWENTY-ONE

So Yahweh God made the man fall into a deep sleep. And while he slept, he took one of his ribs and enclosed it in flesh. Yahweh God built the rib he had taken from the man into a woman and brought her to the man.

Genesis 2:22-23

> That leafless *tree* against which Adam sleeps prefigures Cross,
> Like Haman's. No moth no beast is pinned, **and Adam's** in
>
> His *prime*. So fitting Eve *is called* forth from His rib! The child
> *Herself* is purity, a wonder; no *hatred, miscreance* in sylvan scene
>
> For God Jehovah, looming large, is gentle Master of a yellow
> Beard! So *urgently* benevolent, as if *all* turmoil's spent, a *proper*
>
> Gott *that's lent,* and now compassion! Here *Yahweh's* calm, *if*
> *Such can linger* on. No oak, no *hammer,* subtle, torn, *no nails,* no
>
> Thorn, *shriek,* yawn. In time the beard is shorn, *imperfect* **CEO**
> Albeit cannot see it in **the Book,** you'd care to look, no trace
>
> *This* far. At *least of Judas.* Such innocence *is prior to Adam's lapse,*
> **Is Paradise** perhaps, no Fall from Grace, no love misplaced.

TWENTY-TWO

Lastly, he showed himself to the Eleven themselves while they were at table. He reproached them for their incredulity and obstinacy, because they had refused to believe those who had seen him after he had risen.

Mark 16:14-15

Was not enough He'd shown His **risen form** to Magda [from
Whom He'd cast out devils] or even the two **upon the road,**

None would believe them, but then to the *Eleven* at their table;
A radiance they could mistake from none; was *utter!* Doubter

Thomas inserting fingers in God's wounds to *satisfy a lingering*
Mistrust of his own senses? *Whence came* this spritely Son and

Whence His brilliant fire? That Master sure from vast occasion
Certain to all but death He'd come again, *would* rise *from Hell*

Before erupting toward **God's** grace? There at the touch and
Taste of each and every **was** His face. There **His mien and**

Manner, **certain** there, though billions to come would gather
Heads to shake in disbelief. Was truly sad indeed **their** grief.

TWENTY-THREE

Then the serpent said to the woman, "No! You will not die! God knows in fact
on the day you eat it your eyes will be opened and you will be like gods, knowing
good and evil." The woman saw the tree was good to eat and pleasing to the eye,
and that it was desirable for the knowledge it could give. So she took some of its
fruit and ate it. She gave some also to her husband who was with her, and he ate it.
Then the eyes of both of them were opened and they realized that they were naked.

Genesis 3:4-7

What misery burns our heart 'D render serpent woman, that
GUILT itself's menage a trois, dour Dalliance in WHA . . . ?

Where snake coils Tree, a gap in *she,* a cleft bereft of mercy!
And note transfiguration *of* the groin commenced with Eve's

Odd God menstruation, furthered every inching into **Lapse.**
The character of Phallus, sin: petals? **Ragged** foreskin? That

Human hang here more correct, *anatomy* to sweat direct, sex
To sect: just eye the act! Investigate Eve's pursèd *cursed* Lips!

And hands of each? Such desperate grips! Lapsed **fruit laps**
Tips? Is Scripture's trickster's merely slut? Perhaps awaiting

Satan? The script here **gorges** cut and root, God's rage to
Boot, from grossly grim to Stabat Mater! Quasi Jesu Satyr?

TWENTY-FOUR

Then he ordered them to get all the people together in a group on the green grass, and they sat down on the ground in squares of hundreds and fifties. Then he took the five loaves and the two fish, raised his eyes to heaven and said the blessing. . . . . They all ate as much as they wanted. . . . . . Those who had eaten the loaves numbered five thousand men.

Mark 6:39-44

That first occasion Jesu fed the masses were 10 **thousand**
Gathered to receive, *and fed indeed* by discourse *if not victual,*

Though all indeed by dusk displayed odd greed. *"Dear sire,
We'd need some hundreds* gold denarii *to defray* the cost, *and here*

You'd have us draw full measure from *the paltry sum* we've *laid
There at the base? No matter power will can't erase impoverished."*

25

"Come, men of little faith!" replied *the Master,* spreading graceful
Hands above the weave. *"Reach in, it shall suffice."* That close

Of day the thousands ate their full. And **none** complained
And none was ill; they ate their fill! Even the evening WAS

Truly celebration, a hand of warmth on belly, thighs, some
Miracle of sunset for their eyes—**indeed** they ate their **fill.**

TWENTY-FIVE

Israel, your people may be like the sand on the seashore, but only a remnant will
return. A destruction has been decreed that will bring inexhaustible integrity. Yes,
throughout the country the Lord Yahweh Sabaoth will carry out the destruction
he has decreed.

Isaiah 10:22-23

WHAT **TART** is this to quake Isaiah's heart? Or **brighter
Face** observes from grace? To shake his thoughtful **Calm.**

This prophet's only mildly stirred, has lived the Word, the
Crimson leak of God the Son! *"Come,* quiet in my *chamber,*

*Lad; I've had enough, I'm simply had; or stressed to think, 'D scent
Derision. This prophet tills some mournful fields. Some message this,*

A child's he wields, or wiles a whiles *from* wench to wrench, *a*
Greater *Master's blanch or leafless Tree. This miser mines a* larger

*Misery, some billion billion souls in pain, or gentler rain on blossom,
Root, from mystic shoot to quiet prodding. Your God is* **Godding.**

I seek the **Oddling,** *no small mensch as thee, no savory* **Three,**
Biblical as bubbles in a hiss? Come kiss? Absurd!" The **Word?**

TWENTY-SIX

Mary said to the angel, "But how can this come about, since I am a virgin?" "The Holy Spirit will come upon you" the angel answered "and the power of the Most High will cover you with its shadow."

Luke 1:34-35

> **Enunciate** Annunciation? Luke's **preface** hardly stirs the
> Deed. 2 thousand years contrive to bring us closer, 2,000
>
> Years fruition come to seed. Mary, sweet innocence, there
> Out about implanting usual field, in hurry reluctant leaving
>
> Work as storm approached, a time to yield, thus hastening
> Past **the stubble** of an elder year, there striding home, she
>
> *Paused* at apple tree. What surge so sudden this, what bent?
> As if magic potion lent, so giddy the maiden *went,* unsteady
>
> Knees, *and knelt* and lay as if *to somehow* please some newly
> Rendered force, some urge and shudder for sudden came
>
> Upon her. No rape was this, all proper honor, full wonder
> There in the stubble, grass and *dust, a fructifying* virgin lust?

TWENTY-SEVEN

Then, rushing out to the men, [Bagoas] . . . shouted, "Those slaves have duped us! One Hebrew woman has brought shame on the House of Nebuchadnezzar. Holofernes is lying dead on the ground, with his head cut off!" When they heard this, the leaders of the Assyrian army tore their tunics in consternation, and the camp rang with their wild cries and their shouting.

D.A. Vid

Judith 14:16-18

      Judith and her maid heft General's head, a spasm, bloat on
      The rumpled bed his arms and legs akimbo, neck a carmine

      Leak *erupted into* Hell from swinish sleep and likely satiation.
      A caste of ethical frustration, sweet Judith *having traded* soul

      And flesh for a bloody wayward King! Even lust for least, a
      Drunken feast, that Ding an sich, that greatness? And **then**

      Those nights spewed prayer aloft to God Jehovah, fasted to
      Fell a Prince? And lout he was, **massive** bearded toad, odd

      Slight wench he rode, no maidenhead! For widow ***she*** was
      That wedded fact the *dazzling* proudest daughter of her act

      What courage that *[no slice suffice]* tryst with bearded tyrant?
      What zeal? *for gentler* **sex** her charm, *what* **hex?** *fierce Tigress.*

TWENTY-EIGHT

Then he took Peter and James and John with him. And a sudden fear came over him, and great distress. And he said to them, "My soul is sorrowful to the point of death. Wait here, and keep awake." And going on a little further he threw himself on the ground and prayed that, if it were possible, this hour might pass him by.

Mark 14:33-35

      In the garden Gethsemane, He lies prone into soil, utters
      3-fold *the prayer: "Dear Yahweh, if You're there, incline a loving*

      Ear, I am betrayed! Let this cup pass Me by. Yet let it be as You,
      Not I would have it." And Gott? A silence! *"Let this cup pass*

Me by. Yet let it be as You, Not I would *have it."* And Gott?
A silence! The scent of broken earth, a fragmentary birth.

The darker, sucaryl taste of blood. *They have eaten such since*
Selfsame Flood. "Dear Yahweh, if You're *there . . ." Perhaps my*

Lapse. This band of followers *sleep again through all my pain. I*
Pray, or speak? Again. Iscariot leads the way. My thought simply

Him today; what less can misery say? He eats his ration. And turns
The others toward themselves, his passion. **They** *clamp* my hands!

TWENTY-NINE

"Awake, drunkards, and weep!
All you who drink wine lament
for that new wine: it has been dashed
from your lips. . . . .
Mourn like a virgin wearing sackcloth
for her young man betrothed to her.
Oblation and libation have vanished
from the house of Yahweh."

Joel 1:5-9

This Joel breathes fire bleeds ash and coal**, a conflagration**
Of *the* soul, ragged shriek, no edge hard on. FOR prophets

Thrust with heady brawn, a Braille of man's release, a Grail
Of tease. Proclaim heart's ache, and oven waves perdition.

No whimper blanches soul from whisper's sister, crone or
Gaol, a stitch, a catch. *Deprives its* lives. All *type* belies. 'Tis

Judgment. For goody's gaudy *fodder-larder.* Nurture guards
Her *crimson* leak of which few temperate men might speak,

Just such as Joel, from curst to banter, NO **fond** intention
Coilèd at her. *"A Lordly matter, Justice, trust us,"* Joel *repeats,*

Repeats, ribbed jets of ice, the nails and slice, the wounds,
The lamentation. Here thus the **end of even,** even **Eden.**

THIRTY

But Jesus, aware of their thoughts, made them this reply, "What are these thoughts you have in your hearts? Which of these is easier to say, 'Your sins are forgiven you' or to say, 'Get up and walk'? But to prove to you that the Son of Man has authority on earth to forgive sins,"—he said to the paralyzed man—"I order you: get up, and pick up your stretcher and go home." And immediately before their very eyes he got up, picked up what he had been lying on and went home.

Luke 5:22-25

They were stalled then at *Capernaum in a* mass that numbered
Thousands, had sought refuge in a farmhouse to eat what

Gave of supper, the boisterous mob *crowding* even the very
Door: that no one could come in. Among those sheltered

With the holy, several strangers, *Pharisees and scribes* **who'd**
Prove their *skepticism* had *foundation,* much **as Jesu** *guessed;*

Voices on the roof now being *parted* at the southern edge,
And then, a view of evening sky. *"Here, Jesu,* is your son,"

The *voice* that *greeted from* above. *"Your paralytic son."* Christ
Knelt. *"Child, your sins are now forgiven!"* Blaspheme to *common*

Sight? "In sanction of God's gift, stand now and walk!" Stripling
Gathered *to try the door* what's more depart; **was** *pity.* **Or?**

2014-17

The Gospel of Buonarroti Canto four

If you've read something better,
Chances are I wrote it.

D.A. Vid

BC [the chapel ceiling]

AD [his choice]

THIRTY-ONE

It was in the six hundred and first year of Noah's life, in the first month and on the first of the month, that the water dried up from the earth. Noah lifted back the hatch of the ark and looked out. The surface of the ground was dry!

Genesis 8:13

> The multitude of stricken souls endure the boil of Nature,
> This Biblical abyss the angry Flood. Some cling to Tree or
>
> Stir of mud, a shallow skiff, the Ark that drifts in guise of
> Thwarting Temple just beyond them. How came these 60
>
> Souls to struggle [or Noah secure upon God's covenant]
> For higher ground, fitful pursuit, a *sagging ancient's* breasts,
>
> Unfit to succor wailing child, a lad upon a leafless branch,
> *Scattered* youth and age upon that hill, who cling to useless
>
> Hindering possessions, a Lost's obsessions, dinnerware &
> Table, *individual* partner, female *Cain to Abel,* beyond their
>
> Lot an elder with his son? as if a pilgrim bound to Calvary,
> *A Christ, a* slave, and *slavish haste and rage,* a *gathering* night.

THIRTY-TWO

And all at once there was a violent earthquake, for the angel of the Lord, descending from heaven, came and rolled away the stone and sat on it. His face was like lightening, his robe white as snow. . . . "There is no need for you to be afraid. I know you are looking for Jesus, who was crucified. He is not here, for he has risen, as he said he would."

Matthew 28:2-6

Magda and her Mary climbed dust to greet the cave where
Master rested. Surcease of sorrow had they quested, laden

With linen for a battered corpse. Hours *of incessant* wailing
Had left them hoarse, and yet they cried again *no,* shouted

At a tremor of the soil, fear IN their soul to glean the rock
Had shifted and *there? A holy* being *lifted* to somehow stone

Itself, so bright its face so white its gown? The guards' last
Trailing moan in their haste to *vanish,* as if the very caste of

Death were *banished albeit smile* itself would calm the planet
Or Satan himself would cease disease, *bright beacon slashing*

Swath through endless dark. *"The child you seek is risen.* No
Longer seek him in yond chamber. The reign of *Christ begins."*

THIRTY-THREE

Noah built an altar for Yahweh, and choosing from all the clean animals and all
the clean birds he offered burnt offerings on the altar. Yahweh smelt the appeasing
fragrance and said to himself, "Never again will I curse the earth because of man,
because his heart contrives evil from his infancy. Never again will I strike down
every living thing as I have done."

Genesis 8:20-22

Youth and elders Noah himself each gathered for a *holocaust*
Of yearning, a grateful grace of carnal incense burning. To

Sky shot smoke & flames as Abel alone had pleasèd stern
Jehovah. *Full manner* of domestic strain was sacrificed, fed

To fire, the noble scent suffusing air and gaining waste; no
Haste was here this willful cerebration, where lamb himself

Was duly slaughtered, from son to *daughter*, cleanly best, from
Beast **to breast**, *full ram*, sweet ewe, *the* **blood** *of goat; smoke*

Gathered IN their throats and scorched their lungs. LEST
Disbelievers waggle *tongues*, the Gott of Judah frowned *His*

Pleasure, or smiled to see God's work so freely given, this
Stink of heaven; no bread was leavened, no **s**hrug to **altar.**

THIRTY-FOUR

*Now on the eighth day they came to circumcise the child; they were going to call him Zechariah
after his father, but his mother spoke up, "No," she said "he is to be called John." They said to
her, "But no one in your family has that name," and made signs to his father to find out what he
wanted him called. The father asked for a writing-tablet and wrote, "His name is John." And they
were all astonished. At that instant his power of speech returned and he spoke and praised God.*

Luke 1:59-65

The greatness of Baptist John welled from very fetus itself.
A *fright* had left *him* crippled in his speech a*nd* ambulation:

Zechariah, man to Elsbeth, sire at last to John, but countered those
Who'd call his son by self-same Zechariah, gaining again his voice, a

Miracle *itself: the lad, for his dam was well past* 50. *It settled that*
The boy was *cousin John. Was said* that unborn children *each*

*Conversed while yet in belly, so impatient to be whelped, that mother
Herself gave words to tongue, each discourse by nature holy* in itself,

That volumes of epistle claimed a shelf, were given Script. 3 months

And John, the *coming Baptist, squalled his entry to* Mankind, &

Nearly burst from navel gained true speech; that father at
Circumcision had *voice in turn, each trait so* odd *a witch's* **burn!**

THIRTY-FIVE

Noah. . . . . drank some of the wine, and while he was drunk he uncovered himself
inside his tent. . . . Shem and Japheth took a cloak and they both put it over their
shoulders and walking backwards, covered their father's nakedness; they kept their
faces turned away, and did not see their father's nakedness. . . . In all, Noah's life
lasted nine hundred and fifty years; then he died.

Genesis 9:20-22

> This Father of a cleansed *and coming* age lies drunk to death
> SCENT of new wine? upon his wasted breath, & NUDE,
>
> Flagrantly nude, uncovered, a parody, it seems of Adam's
> Languid pose when quickened by the force of Yahweh, a
>
> Nakedness somehow repugnant *to all three?* to Ham, Shem
> Japheth themselves quite *scantly,* oddly clothed and edging
>
> Backwards toward their Father. Much like Adam himself,
> Noah will face the coming era, but *quite* in error, ashamed
>
> At his 'old man's folly.' So flagrantly subject to idle glance
> With nowhere to reclaim decorum of a sage, enraged to lie
>
> Thus splayed *flagrante delicto,* whose proper stance was calm,
> Contrite, *dignity* of elder, a *drunkard now expos'd* in his shame.

THIRTY-SIX

As for the leaders, they jeered at him. "He saved others," they said "let him save himself if he is the Christ of God, the Chosen One." The soldiers mocked him too, and . . . said, "If you are the king of the Jews, save yourself.". . . One of the criminals hanging there abused him, "Are you not the Christ?" he said "Save yourself and us as well."

Luke 23:35-40

> Even moth pinned *to a leafless tree* endures harsh pain, what
> *Then the Christ?* Even *Haman, hanged, lost blood,* excreta. This
>
> Son that bore the Cross *convulsed in fire and* ache, a blinding
> Wrench from skewered palms, *all perforations* leaking lymph
>
> **And scarlet juice.** But worse far worse, even the vandals
> Taunted this good man who failed His God. "*Eli. Eli, lama*
>
> *Sabachthani?*" And God *was quiet! Inward* wrenching *[though*
> His hands *burned daggers of unending* **loss** and *jagged question]*
>
> Was the worst. *"This Son of Yahweh* cannot save Himself!
> *Ach Gott, His scorn and now He's finished." "Jesu, climb down,*
>
> *Ignore the spikes. We'll worship even your very scabs, leak, stench*
> *You've shat." "*𝔉𝔞𝔱𝔥𝔢𝔯 𝔣𝔬𝔯𝔤𝔦𝔳𝔢*; they know not what* 𝔱𝔥𝔢𝔶 𝔡𝔬."

THIRTY-SEVEN

Again I raised my eyes, and this is what I saw: a flying scroll. The angel who was talking to me said, "What can you see?" I replied, "I can see a flying scroll; it is twenty cubits long and ten cubits broad." He then said to me, "This is the Curse sweeping across the face of the whole country. . . . . . . I am going to let it loose . . .

to enter the house of the thief and the house of anyone who swears falsely by my name, to settle in his house and to consume it, timber, stone and all."

Zechariah 5:1-4

> If naked awkward Popes to come, chapel itself were ruined
> For *Zechariah's* wielding: he *whose greatness* furthered Michael
>
> To endure the grope of such an *Undertaking*! Even Francis
> Of a purer *humanistic* bent, God-sent; no warrior in all but
>
> Purity, the boon of Christian come and gone. As such he
> Carries on eternal *obligation,* to soul and child, a Saint *when*
>
> Saint is simply quaint, a weft of Papal supplication toward
> The womb, the Masters of the Church *entombed,* both great
>
> And merely *large,* both pure and venal. **Such** *Zechariah* not
> Simply penile, a **phallus** wielder as was Julius, that curious
>
> Blend of avarice and **art, who'd have his** servants **fresco**
> Dark to dark & easily endure Transgenders, Lads, Ignudi.

THIRTY-EIGHT

As soon as they came ashore they saw that there was some bread there, and a charcoal fire with fish cooking on it. . . . Jesus said to them, "Come and have breakfast." None of the disciples was bold enough to ask, "Who are you?"; they knew quite well it was the Lord. Jesus then stepped forward, took the bread and gave it to them, and the same with the fish.

John 21:9-13

> Lilac Light was on the Water, / But their net secured no fish.
> **Glitter** of carnal **warmth,** yet / Not a fish. They had cast all

Nets in Vain. The Man Had / Shown Self twice; the Vision
Was on Ice. What God Had / Died? Why return? That we

Must burn? Why His return? / There! There On the Shore!
Once more. I'd have us cast / A net. Not Yet, sweet Lord,

Not yet. Ah Net! We Scant. / The fish take to it Abundant.
Swath of light, a silver sliver! / Lake of Tiberias. So **furious,**

All Moon'd Languish, *Swoon,* / Implore scarred SUN Return!
Beg God's Son to *vastly burn,* / Wade **past,** attach the Master;

Attach at *last a Master's* **past?** / Wade past a net so richly cast.
John's son feed my lambs! **Fishy** /*Supper scent doth reek my* **hands!**

THIRTY-NINE

Saul [said] . . . "Tell David this, 'The king desires no settlement except a hundred foreskins of the Philistines, for vengeance on the king's enemies.'" His servants brought this message to David and he was delighted at the thought of becoming the king's son-in-law. The time had not yet expired when David rose and set off, he and his men, and killed two hundred of the Philistines. David brought back their foreskins and counted them out before the king so that he could be the king's son-in-law. Saul then gave him his daughter Michal in marriage.

1 Samuel 18:25-27

David, poet, **peasant,** King, fornicator to extreme; lops off
Goliath one sure stroke, **trimmed** cadaver, Christly **scope,**

Lineage linked to oddly Adam, cuckold Joseph, weary *adman.*
Leda's Swan were *subtler* prize? Savored Savior *whelped to size.*

Princely neutered in Donatello, elsewhere in Michael massive
Metal. Godly Psalter to a *rooster's* cock, Bathsheba's booster.

Common stock, wenches wider even *Saul could udder, Solomon's
Father?* Tale were utter! *Wedged* the fellow in a terror's tree,

Foliage stouter than the touted 3. **Accident about** to BE?
Route to justice certainty. David a tale, entails bold Adam.

Hands were clean, *the matter* God. Look *too close,* 'tis sadder,
Odd. *Compute the **loss?*** Passion obscure, an ancient Cross.

FORTY

Then he took them as far as the outskirts of Bethany, and lifting up his hands he
blessed them. Now as he blessed them, he withdrew from them and was carried
up to heaven. They worshipped him and then went back to Jerusalem full of joy;
and they were continually in the Temple praising God.

Luke 24:51-53

A wonder **blazed** ascent on sylvan wing. So taken by the
Greatness, knelt the **very Earth,** for merely carnal scant

Endured the thing. Was rare the naked body of the **Lord,**
As *threading* into sky He spiraled *true.* No more was I than

You, and each of us *ennobled to* behold transfigured Vision.
Ecstatic gold *burst* from our lips. There, soaring into ether,

Bold transcendence tore to taste the caper. All bliss *would*
Summon bliss to heed such vapor. I'd beg of stern *Jehovah*

In his mercy kindle this small verse. We're **left** *behind* though
Soaring: brittle, worse. A *billion* suns exploded on the path

He raked. And each of them **unequal** to His Face. Word
Reaches us He's *stationed* King of Kings. Let such *be* such,
the

Mystery stings.

WORKS CONSULTED

Alighiere, Dante, *The Divine Comedy*, Various Translations.
Barnes, Bernadine, *Michelangelo's Last Judgment: the Renaissance Response*, U. of California, 1998.
Buonarroti, Michelangelo, *The Sonnets*, Various Translations.
Colonna, Vittoria, *Sonnets for Michelangelo: a Bilingual Edition*, U. of Chicago, 2005.
Connor, James A., *Michelangelo's Last Judgment*, Palgrave MacMillan, 2009.
Forcellino, Antonio, *Michelangelo: a Tormented Life*, Polity Press, 2009.
Hall, Marcia B., Ed., *Michelangelo's Last Judgment*, Cambridge U., 2005.
Jones, Alexander, General Ed. *The Jerusalem Bible*, Doubleday, 1966
King, Ross, *Michelangelo and the Pope's Ceiling*, Penguin Group, 2003.
Panyard, Christine, *The Sistine Chapel: a Biblical Tour*, Paulist Press, 2013.
Partridge, Loren, *Michelangelo: The Sistine Chapel Ceiling, Rome*, George Braziller, 1996.
Sanzio, Raphael, *Raphael: the Complete Work*, Harrison House, 1969.
Vid, D.A., *Biblical Fictions*, iUniverse, 2010.
Vid, D.A., *Last Judgment*, iUniverse, 2013.
Wallace, William E., *Michelangelo: the Complete . . .*, Universe, 2009.

2014-17

Stacked Rhyme

"I have absorbed, dear God, and transmuted
everything you have given me,
even the ability to do it."

D.A. Vid 1968

A Gallery at **77**

HAMMERKLAVIER

Adagio sostenuto. "I cannot hear the pain!" Andràs, D. Dubal
Both find it there; the whole world finds it there; I partially deaf

Experience simply beauty, stutter in my hearing throat a shudder
As I scan the Purgatorio, Tara's drawings just beyond a spindled

Disc. A quiet agony? Soulful decubitus? Tic douloureux? Mad
Fit of wondrous continence? "I **cannot** hear the pain!" Event?

We skim the final movement. This poet's mute. No visual truck
Or trick to ease the passage beyond the very dazzle real as any **I**

Ever assailed to mastery. **106** remains a stubborn mystery. **10**
Thousands hooked, **mesh** of jagged labyrinth, a ghastly **burden.**

Even a suppliance at the polished boots of Warden **cannot** jerk
Or **treble** cosmic boardroom. Am trapped in "gorgeous, APT!"

AUM

Hectic dialectic: a Gott is torn and healed upon this rack. Heaves
Father Mother Son. Each thrust addresses, spurns the other. An

Ache scream **spew.** Such God is **you:** tangled umbilicus, radiant
Cord, spittle, clot, persistence scrofula of birth unending, **whine**

Wine, attack. Each cyst insists. Slash **ordains.** Gordius **wails** this
Knot. For Gott is caught, all path **taken,** an aching wakening, **id**

On earth. No dearth of birth. Triptych of stare eyes fickle Eden.
Our Eden's **eaten.** But sprouts the center. Such flouts immortal

Cantor. We lick unleavened. *The* Church-lurch-synagogue-temple
Tempi's frozen. Decubiti in Stalin's flank are *frankly chosen.* **Odd**

Syllables retract; this swan is on its back and Leda tickles. Thrust
Fahne under. All sickly's sickled by the Kochs & gilt's a wunder!

AUM II

Creation begets; Preservation endures; *Transformation* remits**;** *aum*
Restores: generative cough of a cosmic whore? **Thesis invents;**

Antithesis preserves; synthesis transforms; aum informs: 'tis primal
Gesture [fester, cluster, Ester, Schwester]. *Rather the dance of* carnal

Motion, such the potion, cold devotion, **such** her rapture, **verse** or
Chapter? To breathe: & summon *Pollux, Castor, eye each wrinkle oddly*

Cast there? Jesu imbibed his cup of blood, asked his Maker *was* or
Would? Coming nails to eat his *hands an opted plan,* forsaken, man's?

A **God's** *demand?* Virgin *mother,* dangling fetus, *Church's fell search for*
What defeats us, wrought salvation cruel and hard. Eye the chapel

Burn the bard. *Father, Mother* even Son, *Godly shun; a Hegel's faking.*
Priestly catch needs *subtle baking*: lick the lesson, **baste** the aching.

AUM III

So many inattentive light-years racked with pain. *Bodhisattva smiles?*
Place of eternal bruise this being we name Earth! Here is all birth!

Dialectic swoons at Gott's deception, that wakening to an ache is
Godlike seeing. The trinal rack is what one makes of evolution, is

Beatific path of endless solution, weeping the calmest center. We
Sense his bent there, wicked Christ. Here! Precisely here is carnal

Summons. Suffer *our* children come unto Thee. *Sweet endearing font*
Of poetry! The movers of his vision simply muse manure, glazed

Ceiling. 'D have us wound the summit. *Feed even the crippled sportive*
Stasis, Godless enrichment, stench the basis. Koch cooks an amp,

An imp, 'D lick the platter. Blond mane is sane no matter. We reel
With *obscene* chatter. We siphon odd Deity unto bruise. **Such** use!

AUM IV

What **focus** could thwart the very horror of incarnate ingestion?
Whose mantis-like suggestion? Impeccable *matron stoop to* devour

Her fetus? Such notion feeds us? How sad the sonnet *of gnashing*
Teeth! Where dwells a soul that fails to seethe? 3 spirals lock us

In a God-some belief. Such is the hectic, dialectic. Such is attack.
Such is the rack. Tender to take it back. *Primordial fact. Look aside*

The image lingers on the eyes. **I**mmaculata spreads her thighs? Or
Conjures a role for wayward metaphysics. *Reduced to excreta modern*

Physics? Cloud bursts and *rain descends* more vacant than pebbles
On a deaf man's roof. Ludwig's aloof. Opus was 106. Über his

Paramount tricks. Conjure a glad impairment? Such has the stare
Meant. Mad *vivisection. Godly dissection.* Painless defection. ***AUM!***

HEAD OF PIERRE...

Rodin, captive to the center, made bruise the texture of his vast
Life. To stroke an aging breast, one must live a wife, or find all

Being in the given strife. To suckle cow, one **cheers** as well his
Steer. In the pasture of disaster bloom the very blades to bend,

A confession Essen, a well of drunken thirst. AUM is clarity of
Water first. "Grant us the wisdom, Lord, to choose what **must**

Exist." There are countless smiles of the same twist. Breath Of
Blossom, nectar's awesome. AUM is a **gift** without **an audible**

Sound to its leader in **106**. Gift is the **rift** that heals all division.
Graft of revision, yard of the curtain, passive but certain, oddly

Diversion fused to the given fact, roar without *tact, shout seldom*
Sought, bartered, or bought, canceled or caught: *IS without Not.*

DOUBTER [CARAVAGGIO]

Merisi spares no hook; ensnares us. Finger penetrates all flesh as
Son guides wrist, intent in lowered glance toward Thomas in the

Very clutch. A pale of chest accentuates carnal obscenity of act
As if nipple itself seems ravished by intrusion. Disciple rakes or

Rapes Messiah's chest? This Gott were misstep crept from Hell!
Delineates each crease and fold emergent from damnation. Two

Witness pair's mutual desecration, 3 hands, a carnal feast of rapt
Apt proclamation. Come Tom, impeach your being in **my** breast

That 20,000 years can assert this spot of ugly wonder. That death
Of Mine holy infernal blunder? Have innards even absent from a

Soul? Let none impeach the title, chapter, "Three days to molder,
Stink, ascend." **Gott** calls me Hence! To Fit of flesh? **Contend!**

FRANCIS BACON

No **large** portion of this face would scare the devil into Church.
And yet it **oddly** competes with his debut study at the **base** of a

Crucifixion. **Nor** derives its manner of mortal solace from teeth
Protruding buttocks in one openly wounded stare. Some welt of

Sustenance is there. *Eyes mimic mouth,* which has *sucked* on inked
Old moral, moribund cosmic **teat.** Face itself is battered by the

Chiaroscuro light that'd have the bard of roadkill naked **all** or **no**
Man to endure. Fantasy regards beaded rose saliva's dribble from

Weak chin, a trace of jowls, bagged *EYE*, mute howls, imbibing
Our certain death furtive in fashion, a guileless stink in a lineless

Focus of eye's mate. No *chance* that one's irate. *Our* quarrels were
Among a captive crowd *this Francis* raked. **Gott** had them quake?

BLAKE'S HELL

A strange and malleable Good Friday here with Dante and Blake
To assess my sins of Omission, a greater gap than my contrition,

Neither untold wild or meek or mild but lesser cause-effect than
This cosmic CEO enduring pain so direct it purses pinch of lips,

And lands him in a *hellish* bracket, **earn a** to Inferno, gaps two
Incisors, swollen tongue parched glance, CA drouth perchance,

Orbs *ohne* iris, glistened nose, flush meaty visage, a mealy mirage
Cooked to serve an inner speak *[Truly blessed **are** the meek]*, from

Closure *to* foreclosure stock to debit datum sheet, *full* merde the
Market in retreat, a spell of doubt, a knell of doom, from cubicle

To corporate corset this damnèd broker without salve to soften
Taxes halve God's wounds, sniff boardrooms, **fright** the **faxes.**

DANAID [RODIN]

At 2 AM I woke from listening gently to a friend who severed ties
Years back. Ron phrased me of the death of his beloved wife. Her

Terrible bout with pancreatic cancer. "I grieved her passing. As if
She'd murdered me our wedding night." That bard's accustomed

Harshness ebbed to gestures of a mild professor, celibate, and she
His Shirley? somehow Danaid weeping strands into marble **block.**

Jean Escoula for Rodin sculpted 1 [50] wives, somehow removed
Ron's cruelest weight, a struggle to get it right, the 49 of 49, **sons**

Of a brother smothered by her being. As there **being** no time to
Properly ruminate, I emerged from attic cot to the designated jug.

An old man in **his** parallel exigency pissed fiercely into it and set it
Again on the floor. That much **I** had lost, *sad* to reiterate no **more.**

FOOTBRIDGE [MONET]

Torment of ripe age? Cataracts alone produce a fiendish assault
Of parallel beauty. Loveliness renders **more** than duty. To loom

In bleeding haze against slashing arc 1923, Giverny and Monet's
Willful **vision.** Construct at labor *cost full* impetus at ripping fog

From eyes, to seize the size, receive a cataleptic seizure, **endure**
At leisure the **usual** pleasure jagged, felt, a thirst, a jaguar's pelt,

The flagrant claws, the limbs teeth jaws, a welt of heartache in a
Blur of blossom, penetrated structure fictive, contradictive, that

Ache is blessing, turmoil indulgent in the warp it's stressing, All
Chatter, wail that tale entails, an ancient's final reach, bold death

Impeached. *Odd Nature* conflagrates endures. From seek to treat
Syphilitic sore faction traction transom ransom spirochete spore.

STARRY NIGHT

Copernicus would stab his eyes for murdering the massive. For
Steeple's mute, minuscule against sky's rage or torment's passive.

Even the shaded hills relent a quiet turmoil. Earth boils in pain
And Lucifer endures. We witness simply spores. Yet larger than

All beatific **suasion.** Universe a curse? Or covets our Vincent's
Deluge in the vaster cradle cupping Gott. Is **what** we've GOT?

What one mad soul has sniffed and caught, a Cherubim a fever.
Let Hawkings rot **forever?** This virus in the very **heart** of pain.

Shall wield and *wield again.* The very strain is darkly **vivid.** And
Host responds. Jehovah's **livid.** Where has this impudent goat

Derived its being? ALL marvel at the **scope** of what it's seeing!
Such *odd* ambition captures ***mother*** Night. **Veins** *leak* the sight!

DEAD MOTHER [SCHIELE]

Umbilicus would-shout-aught-doubt's-about, for childlike, fetal all
But large expressive hands demands a fearful bloody surge, even

To *mascara,* rouge, a painted tragic slut under black quilt's *wrinkle,*
Orbit. Ach mother's demise nears finite in an egregiously welted

Shudder. Tri-fingered hand would predicate distant comfort but
Shrieks itself toward some untimely stab, cessation. Egon **gives**

Brutal lapse a secular Madonna nuzzling cancroid crèche. Cheek
Seeps toward darling terror. Our infancy's an error. Worm spits

A masticated fury. This passive passion's furry. Tentacled decay
Shall have its say: "Tread here with caution; this womb laments!

God smothers infants in their alabaster tents; world moans and
Discord's chord intones; all poem is truly eaten!" Cursed Eden?

ROTHKO

Step inside you find **him.** See it wholly's murdering measure, the
Death **of** massive. Soak in brown in blue in green. *Such implodes*

The stack. Stack attacks. At the very end of these, sliced crooks
Of his arms, wielding Gillette, careful of his fingers. An MD had

Him reach no higher than *"his waist" the* balance of its living but a
Waste, his art confined to posters pretty for the masses. He'd Id!

Deify their asses? Coronate the small? When large was all! Had
A dabbler for Schwager turned them into installation, 30 chips of

Dung no larger than a rhino's tongue, most moist most fitly tame
As if such *zeros summed* **the** error **of** a Master's psychic terror OR

Rothko indeed **himself** just *shy of PhD, cunning as ordure, welded to*
Culpable order, no blue just blots, *"Forget **me"** without* the NOTS.

BLUE POLES [POLLOCK]

The guy that did this was in pretty rough shape. In fact, if story
Has it, 2 poachers worked upon what ended in Australia. Where

It rests content despite the misery in its birthing. A Jackson that
Whelped its final completion was wild man, died so. It wasn't yet

Winter and the Cadillac was of beauty, one of which went to **her**
Untimely death. [I'll *catch* my breath.] I count 8 lovely, blue-black

Poles from the board he marked it with in an instant of supreme
Sanity. He had been filmed at it years prior in his vanity. Tangle

Of labyrinths litter the glitter. Yellows emerge like script. There
Are grays and eggshell pastels, quite prominent. He wasn't merely

Lounging on his fundament. Had I means 10 billion might pry or
Pray *it to my attic. Endure* that *greatness? And* **nothing**, *nothing* antic!

LEONARDO

Sweet Gott of mine, what trace of enigmatic chaste confronts
Odd severed kine? Docile. Photogenic. A **pliant** comfort to

Its lady, rumored Cecilia. And she a mystery beyond the *lesser*
Transgressor hand mimics. 3 sculpted *transcendent* snouts, each

Poignant to the Magdalene she wields, no doubt **levels** even a
Lisa's playing field. For which of each'd yield to Master? Awed

Awe odd hand, to heft a brush, and leave scant trace on grace,
Perfection. *A Lass* impales, a sacral blush, *wields* tears, disgrace

Toward any'd summon grandeur toward her quiet impassion'd
Poise. Ah now at the zenith of *her* beauty with decades left to

Conquer. Miss Gallerani, the force of genius bent your hand a
A sculpted *wound* to every source, all witness and his **torment.**

MAGDALENE

Saucy wench of lad slew giants? Na ja source-less sunk wood-pits
Eaten out of grief in a boney frame praying hard for *pliant. Slung*

From tattered soul, from swollen **truant.** Admonition surges past
Wrists to fingertips, knotted chest, drape of expressive rag-braced

Solely **garment.** Waste shade sucks **tears** hot as Lear's for fictive
Cordelia despite a **risen** Christ? 'Tis yet-regret not God or gotten.

Spills from darkest hole a stab of sight no onlooker 'D *bear. Even*
A Yankee edging past who'd had his fun with Donatello's David.

"BY Christ **we** dropped this on Nagasaki! OR dredged IT UP?"
She **lacks** the beggar's cup, appeals from no man. Such **widow**

Wedded **Christ?** Spread comfort to a doomed Messiah? Heart
Cried? Heart lust? Fierce pariah? Passerby? A? Come to *Dust!*

MOZART [D. DUBAL]

Here has him *ernst,* genius toward the close of "Amadeus." That
Bio was a whit giddy, but then even Ludwig Ursa Major twinkies

At requisite distance. To properly entomb I'd dig the latter. Even
Elder's odd approach to inner worm's a *hazard. Liken his thunder*

Mugs a mourning after. What *spews* after startling glamor? Craven
Crepe? Requiem? Rarified beer-fry? The primal missal reads *final*

Severe. Lunging toward geriatric, *officially* graceless? **Each** honor
Traceless? *Even* Sebastian knew decline? Recover? Simply hover?

Boisterous younger lover? *Odder* L.B. too strung to get it up era
Of **his** Solemn Mass, swear it, hear it, even query. Fast track was

Gordian. Fogged by a weary maggot. Chasing *Euterpe,* Wulfi the
Spritely? Antonio'd Salieri? *Beseeching* the fairly? *Quetching* the slyly.

GAUGUIN

Tabescent God's child screams, nay shouts hoarse into void far
Darker than despair. Some 7 yards of canvas sail rough-ribbed

AS very hands that forced it. Center a pale youth's triumphant
Flesh accentuating slack of infant's diapered groin, near absent

Crease or wrinkle. To left a deity, threatening hag there, here, in
About, painfully conversant with transcendence, a youth's sheer

Plenitude, a slash. The latter exudes from blue, if aspic ash**,** so
Innocent of task, hugely rewarded token caste**, such**, a balm.

Meander mender calm, a given. No price is either here or riven;
Gauguin paints stasis *swirling* against itself. *Past Christian* notion

On the stealth. From neural ache to pagan health, **remote** from
Parsimonious wealth **or** venal commons. Greatness summoned.

KLIMT

A vast remove from **Zika** this paired gestation clearly swollen,
Quaintly bare, gilded ornate cousin, no edge quite given tuft of

Foison-scatter to the latter, her willful cerebration, patter. For
What rough beast could assay past or claim with willful brede

This matter, ladies' fructose: gourds, pudenda, or lend a trump
Or limp defender, yield caution to devotion, starker struck **or**

Burnèd 3 beneath the yielding vibrant DEITY a pattern bourn
By usury, the very wealth of either privileged lass, Hope *I or II*

Caught in a flush of maidenhead, such lithely defined, virginal
At every grace from self-involved or coy [*her* face]. Just trace

The guarded in her glance as if we violate *this solemn rumination,*
Defile an ancient motion, *brittle* the matron shatter the notion.

KLIMT II

Just one lush maiden: nay, 6 and counting. Aesthetic cluster has
The choice on fire. Such lust to mate configuration, edge madly

Into wildest anatomic spray. And having the date right, LEAKS
RODIN. But here the image's thin. No segment rules as would

The latter's school. Biographic *rapture* seeks to capture lyric shift
To myth. One plode explodes to tumble of pudendum; a maker

Bakes her; master chef employs a *visual* concoction. Ah Gustav
Where's your heart? Afford no *means* to start? A place to taste?

We rumble in to Klimt. No ENTRY! A silent sentry guards this
Soil. For *soil has* soul! We harbor infinite conversions, a coil of

Absolute assertions. *Each is for* sale but defines no merchant. No
Wit is certain. Planck's constant, Heidegger to Thomas Merton.

CRANE

His verse the pride of Gordius even H. Bloom couldn't whack, took
Blades of a steamer bound *nowhere beyond* the legend, involved **each**

57

Decade seculars'd *read* though most *are fitful* living *if not* dead, a grief
A torment, blaze, a curious dipsotic icy affirmation. Had I space on

Wicked sheets I'd drum doomed pages rubied with grand citation, or
Explication thorny as the clap in his final proposition, **thumped** idly,

Crudely, soundly, lending **larger** soul more myth, periphrasistically
Donne-stung, as, despite the greater *beast*, more eloquently pure than

Perplexed, far certain of his Hart than of the *Gift*. Had he *truly waxed*
Bisexual? perhaps a pretty end, replete with twinkling cherubs hefting

His corse in silver box, adagios trimmed but *birthing,* that vertiginous
Final curtain, *iffer sister Whitman* wistful if exceeded in the bid for ***id.***

DEAD CHRIST

Is it so much the grief of elders, torment in pierced feet, **hands?**
Or rather the stark **virility,** the hyper-realistic cadaver, puzzling

Son of Man? Even the folds gathered at groin proclaim ***this*** male.
A massive chest? The militancy in coiled toes bicep cheek, raking

Fingers. The man is starkly dead, scarred soles to countenance, a
Warrior so hardy hardly **mild.** Suppliant to oddity a child a quest

Who'd dare this faintly Jesus. The ribs the belly, nipples shout. A
Lacerated Psalm's what he's about. 'Tis eloquence *this* necroscopical

Messiah? Viewer seizes fast to such decay? Macho Bent would
Have its way? Toward odor worm to stain we'd pray: carnal heap

A leak is taken? The tomb where such resides were torrid horrid,
Itch or tonic! Mantegna'd whisper wrench, blanch gut, demonic!

2016-2017

Current Event

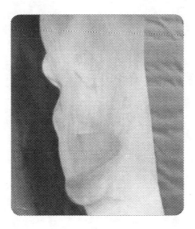

Tara

Very tremendous but lacking bigly.

ISIS

Where dwell our glorious martyrs of the afterlife, what form? Are
Virgins manifested by a beatific presence or alarm? Some million

Such? Of beauty sui generis **or** even singular as Hebraic *heiress*? to
Grace all cherished chiefly rarest? A riddle of the Mariana trench,

Some wealth *of soul* or brute or ghoul (just taste these lips or such:
Is **much!**). What greets a courage severed **Western throat,** or spoil

Of peevish heroic groat (cleaved or fevered; stubborn, **wayward,**
Wrenched **or** savored!). The image chases, bold, reluctance. **Such**

Aspect phrases **dark** domain, a reach for light, unwieldy flight, all
Succored fright, the pit of night, from tentacle to toothy sprite, all

Need, ingestion. *Aesthetics* of the suicidal vest, seared infant, troll.
And weeps to retrain all bliss with cancroid bitch, mute witch, extoll.

TRUMP

This creature buddied up to **kindred** spirits in the Trench**?** Gilt
Kin of sorts, in hassle with the Courts but nominee of **grizzled**

Shirts, who'd lay all blame on "What's his Name?" that milder IF
That racial paradox who blatant *looks* too human to be common.

"LET'S MAKE A DEAL!" the angered squeal—they like the feel!
Of wraith, *Satanic suture,* of solipsistic scoundrel, *Arschloch* **immer:**

Fierce bluster any'd wronged him, ill wrath at any'd stronged him.
Papal-chastened sickly Sect, Trump for triad—Further, Twit and

Hotly bred, *innocent of* solely *Dread*—bigly wiggly, soil'd, extreme,
Putin-pumper, vastly ghastly dreamt, a dream? **Just as I am!** His

Scheme? *Oddly Godly,* manicurist?—pokes excreta's *priestly* purist?
Bawdly gloat, massive Midge: from sludge what else he's groped.

HILLARY

This fearsome docile creature spends her path in current Hell as
Sopsort athwart diaphony, translucent, pliant to the will of elder

Statesman, and yet forthright adrift, adorning cosmic night even
To her innards all the palp that sucks in strength, a blob a clot a

Soul at length, with no cessation from the naked plight—to be is
To be seen, ingest? Surreal between an orifice of splendor, none

To defend her, exuding excreta, a pulse of eat, bright spasm in a
Void of hope, to wield to grope. Attenuated limbs could levy an

Angst *of motion or simply startle. Is* plainest breath this living death
Is mutest spasm. World's udder shudders; she stations at despair,

A microcosm in the willful lack of lick or fret or flick—no edge
Endures mysterious reproduction; mantic cycle? All juice'd idle!

PRIEBUS

An ich *this ugly* rules half the world's Great Power? And though
The grip is stubborn, fierce, it lasts but half an hour? Yea while a

Whiff can curdle blood, can fumigate a prayer [the intent *is* such:
To blast a heart, to rot its veins, and reason, *ethics,* diddle brains],

This febrile Reince shares Death's quiver, quince: its jagged open
Bite, its pinch; his grip's assigned to pus and stink, a *microsecond's*

Jaded wink, lick of ordure, AR-15, all praise to **lustfu**l triggered
Spleen, all quantum riddled, huddled, weak, unclean. Has LIPS

Has clips has NRA, has enterprise, has trigger, fang, has HABIT
Godly quaint, an *oddless* skew, an innocence of gullet, asp to mullet,

Gasp to spew. Satan *Himself* to fry it up? Ask Trump or Isis, *ask*
Medusa; ask boisterous tune, ask **rasp** or ruin, Philip's SOUSA.

A PRESUMPTIVE'S VP

What matter the gender? This IT *is primal* id, a messy table mate,
More wired to savage Essen than confessing. O. Wilde would be

Nonplussed. And where the dentures? Bespeak adventures, one
Hardy quest or inquest margin of digestion. The host? Who **let**

[I **cannot** quit, forget who scanned my invitations] THIS PEST
IN? But HERE'S the Future, wedded to a beast? And seized by

Sutures? Even diminutive white angel angled at forehead crease
Completes the picture. Ach Gott der Adolf resurrects. Or serves

For sex. In darkest pit odd morphs to mute recessive & coming
Führer bites to back the ticket. Snort **deep** to probe the thicket!

You *yearn* to turn back isis? Promote a tactic, crisis? Gorge Eve
With Adam, **STIFF** man**kind**? A **first** impression's often blind.

CORONATION

"How *sweet* these *imperial* mullets, content alone with adoration,
Now advanced to magister and sovereign **to** the Cosmos, **envy**

Of all poor in hearts from anguish exact or whence it starts, an
Ambience so cuddly, preordained, the lithesome chin or comely

Mane oft not visible but always **sensed:** *wisdom mercy, recompense,*
Shudder of Invictus, seed of glory, what seldom creeps into the

Story, a passion faceless as the ample glow from *vaunted mother,*
A God that served her, shed its seed, pulsed its *prouder, whelped*

A **breed** as dauntless as the fabled wires on bearded Jove, one
Radiance that seldom **clove** to lesser Gods, a tabernacle, feast,

All *leftist* notions *void,* deceased." Prost *Trump* or *Pence?* Pomp
Gropes disease. Your sad man's hope? An ancient *squeeze!*

HUNDRED HEADED

How fares He now? This fraud? This mire? How fares His fabled
Heavenly choir? All cant *un-can't?* Or Fact regret? *The simple:* **YET?**

All anger ducked? All **manger** plucked? All rage in **place?** Check
Out His Face! We've bought the image? Or *try* to manage. *In* God

We Trust? Or *game the* scrimmage. Flamboyance **rules?** From Poor
In Hearts to Charter schools? Who *defecates his* **countenanc***ed stools?*

FOR Trump has Trumped the intellectual? The **blessed Meek** the
Godless-sexual? The **Muslim** stench & **grimy** wrench**?** The minor

Miner in his trench. Or factory stiff a lowly clerk the labor's savior:
Promise, WORK? "Ach, it shall come!" Messiah stated. FOR even

JAHWEH celebrated, let not a **tear** fall on his speech OR millions
Gathered to beseech each gesture *phrase,* the COUNTLESS dazed!

BANNON CANNON

A smaller half drives Donald at all hours. If given code designs
Yet Putin glowers. A smiley Goebbels *at his Maker?* If dead not

Merely mute; few could mistake **or**? The FBCIA, emboldened
Golden shower? Minuscule fraction of eternal bite & even yet

Diurnal fright. Amorphous is the lot, a succubus, a spot a clot?
Ach ja, for Bannon fires his Canon, ignores a *Democratic* tic, *her*

Screed or odd infusion. Temporal this Lucifer, for given bruise,
Contusion. We're *headed* dreaded, Lenin-venom, inverted Marx.

Chaos prevails from paper trails to cloud's persistence. A Steve
Entails seraphic churning, incessant lick of Biggest Brother. Or

Hope's redundant. Grotesque's a quest; *the* ethic's *stressed.* Just
Laud the legion's *chest* and dark urea. Sieg's **heil** & culpa's **mea.**

PRO AND CONWAY

Some 20,000 cookie-cutter vamps at His command, Trump seeks
The ultimate sinner-spinner, unquenchable wench unmentionable

Aber-odor: "Ach ja but trust his heart!" Obliquely massive, verity
Impassive; Dummy-struck; presumptive Shrike; a BENT severity;

One cuddly IF from pin to pun, all **get** begot, the lost to # One?
In even Jesu's eyes? **a** smile her style, **no** platitude, **no** stigmatize,

And ode a Bannon-canon, a shirk a perk, repeat reseat, His *abscess,*
Tweet, with scent of primal *Eve,* effete, **be**fore to straddled apple.

But snare makes ample? A jeweler's fenced! **A b**roker's spoken!
Small matter **o**dd's uncertain, from surly, mad *to* blatant, glad or

Listener's Volk *or* media's yolk; or Himmler's brain: **is** smoking?
The tripe's **too** ripe; the sequent smelly? They'd Botox Botticelli.

HEADED HOMEWARD

Flynn flees we're left with whom? With **Spicer** re deicer, gelded
Groom? Which **g**overns such chaotic motion, incompetence or

Grand demotion, flailing seldom seen or heard, State of Libertad
Interred, from *Pence* to *common* herd or griever to absurd, a *Miller's*

Matter, 10 million bused from stoat to yoke for conjured Electoral
Vote. Our ultimatum: governance, testosterone, all maybe-macho,

Groper-reaper, Conway-creeper, mane-mainliner. Who's in *charge?*
The **core,** the base? Who **seeds** the pace? Or **saves** our face? Or

Governs massive hapless **case?** All federal distaste? Our snip and
Paste? **Trump's** taste? Steve's haste? **They'd** have us *even* chaste?

Wisdom waivered, spirit *savored,* treacle *flavored,* bordered, courted?
Or say it's *over* 20 *trillion?* Just read **our** facts. *'D stiff* a *load* of *rats?*

POST MORTEM

O-Donald **T** is safely in His Tower. The Masses'd Lock Him up?
For scandal's bloomed full flower? Some **clamor** for a mug shot,

Some genitalia in Hand. The **total** proceeds just as a **prescience**
May have scanned? They've absolutely found Him out; **'tis** judge

Beyond all doubt. Can mane be chipped? His tax forms shipped? In
Venerable **bulk**, the audit clipped? The FBCIA all hell have sway?

Meander Friend or trender? A massive *orange* Saint's defeat? Salacious
Russians' TREAT in totem? Fearful modem? **Broad** discussion?

Coveted **faux** election? A pall descends on Statute, notion? **Avid**
Eisenhower Reagan *Nixon*? The jury's drawn *with scant* diversion?

Might simply miss the utter person, penchants, rapt excursions?
Grope-hope intrusions. Broad God his fabled trapt profusions.

2016-2017

The Holy City

with "Post-Rumi Ruminations"

[in Charleston, SC]

J.E.Swartz/D.A.Vid

NELL'S BELLY

Exquisitely, sharp terror masks Nell's belly, wound-inclination
Defining such odd texture **I can barely sum** or probe—**Vast**

Utter! Here is masquerade. Quite quiet! Merciful scream? Odd
If love. Sink sudden? The **gape** in *wholly whole*. **Gott** Yahweh's

Pet. Could this absence conjure love and not above—an inner
Thinner itch. What yields must often bitch? Grant dearest! OR

Fairest? All seek *summation?* A wraith devours sensation? **The**
Prey is price? A 3 month kitten? **At 78** I'm smitten. A **stab of**

*Innocence **no measure** can **efface?** The trap I face? *God's grace?*
The cat exists. Jesu resists? Evinces tenderness and pity**? Five**

Months in the Holy City? For *Quaker's* sake a Friend?**—young
Nelly cannot end? She mews assent?** *This* **soul's ascent?**

D.A. Vid

ONE

Master Despair, I stumble through the Dark,
Heft a corpse of God; nothing unusual, odd.

Spit-wet finger of Rumi touches the boulder;
Now lighter than air, it lifts me past the stars.

Where is All's bliss, the broadest smile? **Who**
Tends the Garden? *An Eden racked by* ardent?

Quoth the Christ? "Blessed **are** the Meek for
They shall seek Godless? Protect the **oddest!**

Where are we going *less*? *Tomorrow?* & sprouts
No lesion? Kiss *without* season? *Lips a horror?"*

TWO

Nelly is secretly **attached!** To **Nelly**? Rumi?
Wakes *mornings* to a couplet, **scans C Barks.**

Such cat to **imitate** a dog? Sashay *like a rogue.*
Sniff the Essential, chew an edge, dribble

Her Master off his **ledge,** *Fury* of Natraj, zeal
Of **smoke**, wake to hashish just one toke. **Or**

Monstrous *ego,* gutted Pot, sport a moustache,
Comely act. 'D chase her **mistress into fact.**

Whoreson fiefdom, this and that, **kingdom**
Dasein, *punted,* spat, zealot-pellet, broadly **Cat!**

72

THREE

Nelly seethes for cattle **I've** endured—rhyme
Time No Saint, who can forgive **her** quaint *R*

Ellis trick, that *slack* attack of bric-a-brac *from*
Minor muse to clamor-yammer, one *hammered*

Noisy SOB but **free,** all *latter* matter's perjury.
Who lurks with elder Turks' odd habits, furry

Fury at the *sniff* of fumid formal, triumphs or
Resists *each twist* of *figure,* auditory *chords: Sad?*

An ode? time has *employed,* the *loft* the *leap* each
Lowly creep **from** Chaucer past John **Donne.**

FOUR

Enough of modern verse, all sycophant from
Rage to curse, we shift to Nell's *less oily habits,*

Her cozy up to catnip ploys, her terror *through*
Such noise, what *noise* destroys, all carpet **shift**

Or rare despair or simply *shards (let bards* endure,
All cancroids simmer?) *an* eager flick at what's

For dinner. **She'd** *amble* **past** the *Pope,* ignore
Odd pomp *or circumstance,* refuse each cuddle,

Wayward mood, the ruder homage; erase, *efface:*
Ill *claimage,* indulge tired dodge as *fickle dotage.*

D.A. Vid

HER CHARM

To paraphrase: 'her white: fresh snow upon a raven's back' our
Cat indeed, uncertain breed, acrylic-gray-splashed pristine fact,

Bend in the range of our usual attention, pale rose her snout; if
Woundless hazel eyes to size or through me, 80 short my girth:

4 subtle paws that scan the earth, from tile to kilim, fondle, fret,
Or *test the warmth* or spy the chill from *cushion, spread,* to sudden

Ill, **a mite** of dust, a senior's breast, assorted thighs, their cleft.
For Nelly bravely braves her world in puzzlement heedless of a

Sterner universe, that strange beyond where armies curse, from
Margins weak or insecure, shod pacifist to quest obscure. Nell's

Rover kiss, *remote from hiss,* the latter guarded in a dark recess 'D
Ward off *demons furred or faint;* she'll *age to such* when *much is ain't.*

FIVE

This house is *also* habitat for gentle lithesome
Lisabeth (the *end auf Deutsch* must rhyme with

Yet) for such **is** she, an import sworn **to** deduce
All mystery, though puzzle at **this** moment to

Her spouse (*his crippled* rhyme *an odder* eastern
US crime). So be enamored she the younger set,

Sucker for a toddler, pet, and harbors treasure
Only small folks can't regret, like old Dr Seuss

Or EB White, has **neighborhood** enraptured,
Quite, converging on her street, all *tears'* defeat.

SIX

The **bond** is strongest with her Nell, bereft of
Hell or inquisition, for **nothing clings** to **taut**

Decision, no *jest too subtle* to *decipher* (our Nell's
A Lifer —army jargon). The pair repair to cook

& kitchen lest hubby tight might lend *a bitching*
AS appetite is seldom slight *for* Master's *supper,*

Lunch, no mention fur-food, mother-truck-OR
Snacks from Trader Joe or Publix, Fancy Feast,

To **go**. They pounce they wince and dart about,
'Tis one great *shouted hiss* from Mistress Liz-Oh?

SEVEN

Housemaster **Mark arrives** at 8 PM **ensures**
All have had BM. No direct interrogation; AS

Counterpoint the current nation, mischief **of**
Its wayward *Chief,* escapades that strain belief

If not in God the awfully odd. Settles *down* in
Current seat; much to say **I** can't repeat lest a

Daughter hears report; samples *Elsbeth's* latest
Tort; out in time to lift **his** weights: offsprung?

Caught *her, seldom* prates. Plunges toilet *changes*
Lamp, **offers** hand to **grip;** *lean* as torso, *damp.*

EIGHT

A daily try at CNN brings sly skit to us but *harsh.*
They've *drained* the swamp but slog the marsh.

At least it seems to neophyte; we *bond on much,*
But much is fright: *daily* weather in the whitest

House, massive shuffle of *debrided* louse, **clatter**
Of saucer, leaky plates, *march* of the wicked, if

That *grates,* frantic obscuration of the **heav**enly
Gates. **At** times *a Conway,* Pence, a **Flynn,** and

Overall that *purséd moan, from ruddy orange hair* to
Chin, convinced: your *guess* as *content spin* or grim!

GRAY FRAME

New cooler, stove, new table, chairs—the kitchen is complete!
And love went into it—new-minted daughter, an innocence 'D

Wrought her, helpmate comfort *to a Paternoster,* a mother's child
New coined as blessed, so *sweetly such,* assign or quest; despair,

Compassion's errant brother hapless victim to an ageless other.
Merciless self on Sumter St. lifted a couple *past desist-or.* **Savor**

Of such in bright summation; 56th year swept free and patient.
Currency redeemed in *blossom,* dust to etched Mimosa, *awesome;*

Goddessa, attendant *Demi-Angel* radiant on the second landing;
Survival, growth from mending; wrenching pain to maturation.

Knew bitter ache and knew regret but knew it certain newly met,
A solace given simple deed nor deedless facing simpler **Need.**

NINE

Intriguing **is the** room where **Elsbeth** sleeps
So secretive *the lass* so private, seldom *irate* or

Adumbrate though Fate **has** left **much** on *her*
Her platter: while often sad-or out of sorts.

Often I am **at** last resorts to **sweep her from**
Her chalice toward my water **tumbler,** to kiss

The *maid* awake, investigate *the glitter,* all secret
Ware she **guards** since our arrival in **October.**

Small chance! She *locks out most intruders!* Albeit
Neither *rude nor* tactful: simply firm & fact full.

TEN

Though little *to* reveal or calibrate I'll *spend* an
Extra stanza. No TV there, computer: *the lady*

Reads! And fusses with *her* Nell. Hell's sweet
Belgium *goodies* are secreted by this closet-toss

It diabetic. *Odd* if *not compelling* art-works grace
The **ceiling**. Lower surfaces repeat. **But** nada

Truly nothing there no matter how I squint it,
Either. Behind her *customary* neck's a mottled

Pillow which *denies* prescription. Rumored *our*
Cat hides, threshold further? **If** should I offer.

ELEVEN

How many children did he slaughter? **But** *Dad: they*
Were adults! **170** *Churches in the City limits?* **But?**

My daughter? **'Tis** *better?* **Even,** *worse! mildly* **'Holy'**
Terror? Human **curse?** *Investigate his choice?* **That**

One Child? Alone? Quiet: I **hear** *a* **faint** *atone And*
There **is** *no You? [Beneath the* **2ⁿᵈ** *pew?* **The 3ʳᵈ?]**

In the Beginning was the Word? How many perished
In wordless spasm? Should **I if-has-him?** *Chasm?*

Herrick had it-'Lullaby.' **Why?** *Simply a breath of*
Dust? *Lament? Repent? Relent? In* **God** *we* **lust?**

TWELVE

A **Single** *weapon* **most** *he had? The lad?* **So** *sad!*
Who made **it?** Sold **it?** Bought IT? Ought IT?

What **did HE** hate? **Whom** berate? **Parents?**
Fate? Dished the **'evil'** on HIS plate? **Mate?**

Wait! **What** the Country? **Crooked?** Straight?
Someone *paid* us for the Sermon? Braised *the,*

Raised the *Err-mine?* Simply vermin? *Common*
Term? In ANY language? **Whose** advantage?

Simply dotage? In **whose** homage? *Rummage!*
Black, brown, dun, pinkish-pastel, roughage?

D.A. Vid

GAY FAME

Void Beyoncè? Odder bother. Comely brother? Neither offer.
15—27 Years we lived a Shaker. Janis J? Easily 'D shake **her.**

Must evoke a vocal yokel. Solitary spawned **emissions?** Total.
Emptier bed no given bread. M dug lass? Couldn't last. M dug

Onan? *Cancroid* vermin. Suppèd at her lower portal? *'Dangered*
Chortle. **Vid** at 30? Torment, flirty. **Vid** at 40? Vapid, **portly!**

Vid at 50? Rigid, thrifty. Spawned by Zen at 51. Married once
But wasn't burned. Married chance; am not interred. Savor all

Savior wench'd-or-woman? Prozac, Meth, Zyprexa, **daemon.**
Even Whitman seems severe. Wholly ghost by my *second* year.

Racked by fear. Second year. **Sought my water in the weir.**
Song of Self, monstrous health, **parsimony,** greed to **stealth.**

THIRTEEN

Size legalize. *Secrete* the ration; Clip *the nation.*
A which's brew? *An adder's* lotion? Then who

Or whom? It crowds the room? A patriot or
Patriarch? *God's* Tree **of Life** *without* its bark?

Where is her song **without** the lark? A trailer
Park a **gaited** City? *The* **poor-in-heart** alone

Intones? *We spot* the mantra grief *impugns, ill*
Passive lotion. Or wield the motion. Yield a

*Cau*tion. *Our* Gott can't intervene; *the platter's*
Heaped. Amused? Just Google! Ogle Mogul!

FOURTEEN

Nine corpses litter sanctuary? Most strange in
Guess or fact! All mass attack. The National

Stack? Much broader, odder, in dispute. Some
Hesitate to calculate, some find it chilling; our

Weekly leaking gullet, throat, 'tis too obscene,
A furry screed, a *nasty* bleed. 'Endure *the* fury.'

Dread for dead, each *Dozent,* hurry? No **souls**
Should soil the Sabbath? The Godly *'blabbeth?'*

Suffer the children? Come unto *Thee?* From NRA
To **poetry?** Who've **knelt** *unto* the Anthem?

FIFTEEN

Amerika has **spawned; the** elders yawn. They
Carry on. The taste is bitter. Who hired *infántile*

Baby-sitter? Who screwed the dance? Greased
Her prance. Whored the sour? Glower-power?

Motion potion. Putin-mute-one. Wicked *thicket.*
Waver quaver. Grope **elope.** Fortune *fountain.*

Shape escape. Master mister. Kissed *your* sister.
Photograph? Broadly apt? Thinner lapse. Wit?

Perhaps. *Locomo*tion. Let the roach *in.* Gleaned
The rabbit. Wore the habit? Flayed the Babbitt.

SIXTEEN

On Sumter St I've *learnéd* to distrust my words.
Painter of line detest his Colors? *or lust her* hordes?

Picasso's stare more than a billion Miltons, an
Oath without a look *the* latter scrying Paradise.

For whom was lost, the valance gained, to ink
It such, remote from *touch,* no saint but *painéd*

To justify *God's ain'ts,* promote a febrile vision.
A gentleman of lofty disposition, querulous or

Out of sorts, *hostility of Trumpist with* the *Courts,*
No randy, King James crisp but handy-dandy.

MEETING

12—13 chairs face idle inward in a shabby room, small candle
In a crystal base. In time's measure 9 strengthen toward center

As usual **incomplete.** The gathered observe dark and day, that
Flicker somehow north of futile. Sweet cliché emerges from an

Open sweeter lass I briefly covet: '**so** grateful to be given quiet
In a hectic week.' Off center further intrudes: Then Why must

She **interrupt** it? Eyes mine focus on the candle again there-in.
Where are we going **less** than tomorrow? **What can** she reach?

To teach her sorrow? Where is the center within the sin? What
Has **she** been? Even the knife that cuts a smile? Latter is thin?

Or other? Prim? My **left calf aches.** They break. It is 11 AM;
Chill First-Day morning in the Holy city. Lass **was SO pretty!**

SEVENTEEN

Has this scribbler strayed **too far?** Suffice that
Victims in the wings are thusly treated, their id

Kids seated in the media shooter-throne till all
Attempts at 'justice' are employed, a Holy City

Decently employed that poet can forgo odd ill
Pronouncement. In abstract one can **opine an**

Odd revenge, 365 times rampant beverage or 1
Rude stroke to quell *most corporate* **pain, no idle**

Leverage or announcement. Invite the stranger
In, refrain *from* grin, *the* danger's dun, uncertain.

EIGHTEEN

Every church 10 million saved is savvy for the
Kitty. All types all brands for sanctified or one

Night *stands* the steeples *scratch* an ambient *air*
Or dance *constricted* in the ample *lair* a *Buddhist*

Mantra, Baptist Split, Lutheran, Brethren, *Holy*
Skit, denominations gone but never quit, from

Sermon hymnal, Popish chatter for bless those
Gaunt or simply fatter, the *vapid,* sharp the curt

The saved, or gravid graved or prompt serene
Thin idiom grateful *in* between—**the** Holy City!

NINETEEN

The house is past a hundred, we *not far behind.*
Through most of that I've *hungered,* the recent

Less unkind. Imagine that today *I am* befriended.
Mentor perhaps to genius [or sense its hover].

Future looms in semaphore. **Had known the**
Whore & paid the dues, no Pulitzer no august

Nomination-hesitations **lurching at** the Muse
But here Gott struck far past **facility** *or* **grope.**

An anapest and **juice,** dactylic cipher, trochaic
Writher toward iamb—*with Gene must say I Am.*

TWENTY

I hate to kill **the** promise of a **poem** that **lasts**
Forever, but **have pushed** my **luck** to write at

78. In every TV ad the senior wench is tending
Flowers *while her mate clips bonds.* **'Tis** *well advised*

I find a suitable occupation or a date. The latter
Needs be well-*assisted* blond from *sleek* to Vamp.

Unadorned and *often absent frames* that *might depress,*
Mammary swell discrete and *not foreboding, goading an*

Apt investment, *prudent* medication *stout bouffant.*
Could blossoms never wilt? My wince or **taunt?**

THE GOAT

31 inches from the crimson udders of a primitive black goat, I
Focused on this painting at my progress **into Hell,** distended

Butt-cheek, pairs of flasks, jugs breasts, the latter crimson tips
That flare above belly, pubis, legs' juncture a wide pale swath,

Face featureless silhouette, her left attendant lady's head **and**
Javanese vase, willfully clumsy tilt, all in fact coupled, shock

To my Gestalt in 1962. So friendly are they now, the pairs, an
Odd wide warmth rendered tame in the current ethos. Hopper

James not Edward yet, wed my Hugely elder **sister** who fled a
Fiery start toward Hausfrau in Tucson, on 27 medications, her

Litany of ailments, children dispersed *toward* similar ill measure,
Treasure of **regret** their **set and setting** mercilessly **correct.**

TWENTY-ONE

What **prompts this** child to write again? **You'd**
Greet such dogged effort with a grin? Or find a

Smile, look past your shoulder? Enable Rumi *to*
Loft his boulder? **Induce** a reader clap or **list a**

Grievance? Or ragged, strut, as penance smut a
Sacred **journey,** no *softy* clamor, *diamond, amber?*

The *glitter bitter,* ambience fitter, a *smack* of wine,
A rudimentary *vintage,* humbly choice, *rejoiced* if

Wriggled on the vine, an appetite of graced but
Stout, *derived* from *affirmation,* chased by **Doubt.**

TWENTY-TWO

Greet such *dogged effort* with a yelp? **Find even
Larger soul** at best *regaled?* THIS scribble 'tis

Fur and spit itself**? A wealth** of *health a surge of
Wisdom?* One cannot judge till we've kissed 'm?

Take it as Einstein at his violin? Bailing a boat?
Ignoring Billy Graham? Repenting **Cheers for**

Lost or Silly, inciting Brothers in their cups to
Philly? Scratching sly sinner with a ruddy filet?

Blistering *Sister? What ere it takes* Ignore? *When*
Head of State is buckling under to his whore?

TWENTY-THREE

I hear a crash; she's fiddling with a roach? **This**
Windless city has it thoroughly 'palmetto,' for a

Euphemism. I'll grant you even huge *they're* **not**
A tree [I googled it] *from* psalm to palm, *in unser*

Ghetto. Our Nelly *doesn't* scold *just* chews them
Out; they're minus legs if larger *than* my thumb,

Assessing the cadaver. Smaller of the North are
Found in hordes, these singular, averse to pack

Or crowd. I've turned them up and down quite
Dead inspiring *awe,* chagrin, *plump* or Sjogren's.

TWENTY-FOUR

Such maladies entrappéd my stern sister, *not so*
Nelly. The latter's youngish, fit and longing for

A fracas thus far she's graced **us.** Sweeter, *simpler*
Than a clover, inhaling trace, cadaver, pinching

Catnip vermin, *from which* she'll burst headlong
Through the flat, asserting that she's feline, no

Ante omen. 'Tis *such not random,* phantom, *oddly*
Godly, mystic, septic. Sleeps often on her back,

So secured to comfort *zone.* Dead ahead speed
After aught, whatever usual homely handsome.

MORE HOPPER

Far to my left, beyond a lilac spread 2 sunsets vie for beauty, a
Quietly **vertical** diptych. **Capture beyond** simple **color field**

Verisimilitude, a voice against muted yellow siding, perhaps *the*
Final series of a life. Here blood implies no certain anguish. We

Lean on such, even thirst, willing, despite cruel odds genius in
End stop statement. Deem safely *more of adjacent* vegetation as

Given tender heightened calm, where lovely's **spattered** in the
Tentative pale swath and drip. Never Nature **this** cold charmer.

The dominant chill grays, or subtle imploded shards of stricken
Color? Where has soul gone, if real, beyond? To portrait of his

Daughter facing? Jennifer: vacant eyes-grip-chair-broad-belt, or
Hyper-realistic slacks, **rude** dazzling splay of sunlit **grandeur.**

TWENTY-FIVE

Our prelude [Elly] passed at 21, left heart Hole
Barely *sealing*. Our *current* [Nelly] charts syllabus

Of feeling. Near-her *is lesser* **than** *distraught,* nips
Nonetheless the edges. I have known *no* **mortal**

Fur-friend's *quiet* so endearing. *To park at 3* AM
Her soft *white belly* at my toes, *to thumb* her nose

At odds she could be trampled, design arthritic
Stroke **holistic** charm *no* false alarm, purgation

Simply such, is much! A blessing to our *modest*
Gray-*frame simple* dwelling. Her nuzzle healing!

TWENTY-SIX

My dearest Elsbeth fake-fights her **subtle** kitty,
A practiced **shift** to routine edging **toward** the

Opposition. The Nell advances, leaps and nips
[Just fabric, tear like static], retreats **or charges**

Toward the kitchen, tumid tumble, evasive, AT
Shift to flight **an** *awesome* sight *quite* **unevolved**

From terror. Braided rugs scatter, shift, upend,
Recoil; the silver rattles [stainless *steel*] *a shudder,*

Thrill, the latter Cat-or Mater's Weal, a dish an
Avocado [peeled], Elisabeth's redacted **squeal.**

TWENTY-SEVEN

Is there taste of such paradise in *our* constricted
World? Can shadow dancing of our Nelly lift *or*

Pace just *how* it's curled? Can human *kind escape*
Its dreadful wisdom? Must mouth phrase curse

Before it's blessed them? Nelly exists, a sudden
Fissure in *on-rushing* Fate? Does such odd *beauty*

Ever quite escape? Moment is such, a wealth, a
Scream. Endure *your* lot when dream's obscene,

The now is massive in immortal measure. How
Else HER seconds swell such mortal **treasure?**

TWENTY-EIGHT

The sad perhaps *can texture* limitation, *fouled* bliss
Or kiss or holy. Letter such to leverage much &

Grant the whole transmuted *wholly.* Odd **God?**
I'd borrow word I'd dare to utter. All mortal is

Constricted in the greater Welt, inscribes a godly
Scripture in a *fleshly fault,* most wayward, inked

By Nelly's Judas-Cain's; who *willed* **to** conquer:
Conjure, stain. The *melody* wields *age-old* refrain:

Our smile is fashioned by a twisted knife. Laugh
Endure *through endless strife*? Simply *love* her life?

D.A. Vid

NATRAJA

Faux brass Natraja, God-destruction *dances* in his wheel of
Fire above our clothes rack? while His sullen antipode Vid

[Collected IS his Word] bulks at the other end. Neither is
Anti**pathy** beyond self-achieved, both believed, in the sum

Of God-creation; both counter all **human** limitation, both
Linked *amity-to-the-four-young-deities-diagonal-there* confronting

Hopper. Where Avedon's **idolatry** fuses WIT in a nascent
State, clear-eyed *open* Grace, each face, beneath a frieze, a

Seize, a seminal mortal. Whose voice is given? Whose soul
Is riven? **Who** dwells AS **origin** and summit of Vid's Life!

From whence the **wife,** *the Muse* the *price*? *Procedure?* Such is
Ambition free of leisure. Such is his evanescent *holy treasure.*

TWENTY-NINE

Love paradox, love poor-in-heart. Remand the
Rent before it's dark. Confuse the issue. *Snort a*

Line. **Afebrile** notions? Cease, define. *Trumpĩan*
Mind is muddy gesture. *Reduce* mad *germs* before

They fester. Virgin carrot IS the sanctioned *hue?*
From cheek to spread, it *could be* you. Wrap our

Leader in a mailéd fist. Wrap *son* of bitched **&**
Broadly Twist. 'Tis FIRE and fury that *he can't*

Resist. *Chaucer?* Pasteur? *To pause to* toss-or *even*
Fit her? *Would sink* our POTUS jam his *Twitter.*

THIRTY

God damn it aren't we holy? Remove the scab,
Insert the Foley. The *sanctuaries* hold their own;

Our prayer to God's robust. Ash **Wednesday's**
Forehead smudges **have** their **lot; we've not**

Forgot. The Ninja man is dancing free of cost,
The pastors suitable, discrete. Even *the Buddha*

Chimes; the rappers rhyme; the Citadel's effete
And nudged toward Patriotic glory, salute Old

Gory. A Rumi here would stir a throng; *a lass a*
Thong endures the shores; all *just* gradation snores!

THIRTY-ONE

What hierarchy remands to certainty? What 3
In one what *verity? Access* the doubt in Hegel's

Soul. Blast wind or solar on the lurch to coal?
Who'd scorch the *cosmos,* torch the whole; fit

Thesis? Cease Is? Dialectic hefts the boulder;
A carrot rules, a **Donald** builder. Our debt's

Indebted—sullen-45 *will lick* the fundament of
Strumpet's pride, *will chew* the hide: *some billions*

Deified. *For Morgen rises, hooks* its Cross; ALT
Welt's a bounty; hail loss hail empty, tempest fossed!

THIRTY-TWO

What Gott's name has such to do with Rumi?
'Tis merely Rumination! Air your frustrations!

We're past 300 lines. *Searching* for affirmation!
The means oft justify *the* end. *I bend* the quest?

Put Rumi to the test! A guttural leap deserves
Its pounce. From **sanctity** to curse my **duty's**

Sound! I *crucify* no poet. As if I wouldn't POE
It? Ambition is a muddy lot; we slog [as said]

A marsh. As such fall out from **perspiration,**
Doubt, **who** *succeed? From hex to sex* they *screed.*

MEETING II

So much **affirmed** felt crippled in my **shame. Reveal my**
Darkness? Carcinogen? Scavenging despair? Ebony coffin

OF my heart. But must relinquish so-to-say all thought for
Fragile Nell. Nightly bathroom trip when I confront HER

On my **chair?** *Open* to an elder's tremulous hand & touch.
Is such? Not **much?** I have shouted toward the Void. The

Empty pit betrayal. **Starvation** of a billion souls. **Infants**
Suckling dust. Christ sake? this **blossom's** vastly overage,

Uprooted. Tormented Tree of Life? 'In Adam's Fall. We
Sinnèd All?' Thrust Faith in **fire** to temper. I tamper? Or

Sleep? That rain *today that weeps,* having used my aid? **Tell**
Each and every: our **Collective** curse—**God's universe?**

THIRTY-THREE

Had I means I'd **vest it on the given blond,**
The situation stormy? sadly *pliant:* wrest client,

Livelihood itself, property, the principally *lily*
Oddly purported old, **that** **horny?** GAVE all **his**

Digs, possessions for a sniff **sub-navel,** lavish
Title-august, meretricious, ideologically *hungry*

Prevarications, golden toilet revelations, godly
Pinkel-sink-hole-scrapers for a pair of *youthful*

Bladder-capers; gave holiness itself, disease, *the*
Cure, gave *more, even* less if squeezed, the **tease.**

THIRTY-FOUR

The contortions there seem **hardly** worth the
Effort. Dealing *with such has taken half* a planet?

But trust a soul who cannot endure a cat? I've
Met them. **An allergy** can part one's way with

Most? Suspicious! Just trust *a tortured* landlord.
We went that route. Duffer *suffered!* I held him

Up to light to view his soul. **Somehow** it left
Him in control. I *flushed* his memory down the

Toilet. The scream was piercing. Am *often bent*
To borrow lend an ear. The *torment* **deafening.**

THIRTY-FIVE

The switchuation wormy? Sodly pliant: blest client,
Ear to fear. WHY piddle on *the* poor-in-heart,

Diddle *the last* to start, *incarcerate the* wounded?
My age-old clock's not <u>wo</u>unded. Christ sake,

It's a Timex! Paid up **front** 40, *Change.* Within
The <u>bo</u>unded can't predict the diction; is such

With fiction, **spare me** critic, **the** effete; there
Are churches on this street, a synagogue or 3;

4 nuns a priest 10 hilly rollers, pregnant wives
And jogger-strollers, **city's** Holy. And *he* hollers?

THIRTY-SIX

I've read the weekly Times included poem &
Soaked it into every verse that's second rate;

Just beg me cursed not straight, am **suitably**
Opaque, no common scribbler. If poetry's a

Current mess just get it off your chest, don't
Count me even half of piss-and-moan, these

Things aren't koans. Besides I've *garnered My*
Rejections. Just look at any usual stanza. We

Do our thing! **This** *stuff matters!* You'd rather
Reruns of Bonanza? You frigging Pansy!

NELL ADDENDA

Investigates my room? **Arrives, the cat,** in a blur and thunder,
Heedless beyond a will to sniff, even my keyboard, the tangled

Electronics which connect me to the *planet*. She is at the **blind.**
To scold would **be** unkind: thus far she lacks neurosis, even in

Omen. I have known few *of such health* in **kitty** kingdom. Snorts
Tums, an empty flask, **prefects** this servant of despair, as with

The rest, even as now she hides *beneath* beige spread, hoping to
Engage this poem. Claws at an emptied carton, *approaches* book

Shelf, sinks from sight, emerges with no mute effort *at Heidegger,*
Wedging past Harold Bloom's *'Anxiety of Influence.'* I **admire** *her*

Poesis. *Oblivious* to this *author's, she* leaps to the *hardwood,* **skirts**
M Donoghue, *self-portrait,* 92, the solitary *pastel* **of his** existence.

THIRTY-SEVEN

I pass 360 lines *with no coherent* subject matter!
How current can you **get?** Perchance **an ode**

To Horace, even sadder? Relent your critique
They groom the adder. Cleopatra? Down the *ladder.*

Retire to J Joyce Such **ipso** ancient? Rhymes
Syllabic toward the *center,* skewed but patient,

Even manly Manley Hopkins? Died of TB *he*
Or **hodgkin's?** The crater's *deep* we've *stuffed*

His Muse; she's not amused. *Takes years to glean*
Reaction, and now *polite contrite* & indirection!

THIRTY-EIGHT

I've darkened *the* local *hothouse with* rejection.
Skewed personal taste *lent honest-bent infection;*

Retreated from *the* celebrated norm, opened
My cans of worms to seed the *platter, wrenched*

Sense groped chance, but dodged **the token**
Winner: read *widely* 'major' *wrought, even lesser*

Sought, the *fraught* the humble. See how they
Rumble! Hadn't *acquired* the *stomach to* endure

Such corn *that* passed *for* harvest. Neither pap
Nor *Pope* nor Marist. *Lack spunk for cherished!*

THIRTY-NINE

414 Sumter's *pushing* for reprieve. *Nelly* cries,
Her Mater's out; cat senses mad design. *The*

Stars are less aligned. Would they **willingly**
Resign to leave me stranded? Of course her

Master doesn't matter. Nell has *him lower* on
The charts. Where upon the tasty snacks, or

Puddle of whipped cream, matron's scent if
Time to slumber. She has **his** number. Old

Guy passes muster, nothing sacred. For *who
Translates all gesture into Prayer, is* **every** There!

FORTY

Dear Mahmud, Jesu, Christ, she's back! Not
Simply **there** 'tis back attack. A phantom of

Forget has just expired. Of *course* they'll take
Their nap; *the bed* **is crisp** with linen supple

Scented from *the* dryer. If larger world's adrift
Here's *heavenly* couple. No *gratitude* there-is is

Sadly wasted. Humility is sweet sensation, a
Pampered *life no* hampered cerebration. Ach

JA, *attend the* rite; **'tis almost subtle Night**
A furry *fiery, lean satori. 2 angels wield the story.*

MEETING III

The *window* . . . ach ja ignore the window? Where fronds crepe
Myrtle now past another summit flick flecks of innocent petal

In wind gusts shower-laden beauty past the glass, now clear &
Milky column's glare a *quarter* of the horizontal pane: endure a

Stubborn heart with antipode of grief, all bleed in pain. What IF
Is centered toward infected soul, what such? A stab of blue an

It-caress? *No clinic* diagnoses ill *intent* no gauge no unassuaged
Mortal gravitas no loss no *termination*—this summons: mid-July

A thrust of summer. Such Nell's *clamor* ample grant with ***now!***
Here in a Holy city I center briefly **eternal** bliss-**evokéd** pale

Cascade, now visible culmen of the column's pair's full shade
Alone apparent in a *scattered* motion. **I eat** beyond to satiation!

2018

Surfing Eckhart

< a critique >

Des Moines Register 1970

< in memoriam M. Megraw >

[All quotations are from Matthew Fox, "Passion for Creation," (Inner Traditions International, 2000), sermons of Meister Eckhart, Fox's translations, on odd occasion as noted Fox himself.]

ONE

"The more suffering is great, the more suffering is little, and the more it is like carrying two buckets. The heavier the one, the lighter is the other. The more a person abandons, the easier it will be to abandon. A person who loves God can renounce the entire earth as easily as renouncing an egg." [68]

On route to River Acheron, 45 *gilded* swine, a bleat and ruckus
Seldom raised in thunder or in rain, leech-beseeched, sublime,

In fine hefting smartly gilded *pair pails* brim-wise laden-made-in
USA with gilded ripest rats' eyes, sumptuous salute, the driver

Greetings to Charon, his sturdy skiff, All of Jehovah's misery
Still a lift for pitted hairless thighs. Hail *to the* Chief resounded,

The swine impounded **[each piggy cried**!], their wherewithal
Confounded [a Sharpie log? Of frantic hog?] *the 45th with empty*

Pails, ALL bent for *Wharton School* or Yale's. The river running
Slick, the driver sick with indecision, having run *his life* above as

Curt precision, too late to preen or balance load, more toad or
Prayer required than tanning lotion, than fabled hair, **devotion.**

TWO

"On this account, the more you are able to bring all your powers to a unity and a forgetfulness of all the objects and images you have absorbed, and the more you depart from creatures and their images, the nearer and more receptive are you to the secret Word." [297]

Meister Eckhart heterodox *sought* procreation above Bach's. 10
Billion sons of God *adorn his Tree,* Virgins to the *ilk degree.* Wove

A hair-shirt for the *disbeliever*, countless sightings, instant fever.
Largeness of soulful absence, VOID, princely Paupers, primal

Chord. *Symphony* of *father/son,* mother/daughter, anyone. Pried
His brain toward affirmation, holy self and desiccation. Parked

His mule *beside* the Fountain, *softly shadowed,* massive mountain.
Explications urgent, gummy, holy bread for every tummy. SO

Ignore the venal itch *sin itself* the primal *Kitsch.* Hitch your cart
TO Eckhart's potion, planetary lapse-demotion. Salt by YES,

All *wayward* platitude, proper-lovers, what they chewed. Bury
The bitchy butcher in a treacle soup, dine, resign, in Finitude!

THREE

"If your friend dies, let it be in God's name. If you lose an eye, let it be in God's Name! With such a person, may it be all right. If you are sick, however, and ask God for health, your health is dearer to you than God, and he is thus not your God. He is the God of the kingdom of heaven and of the kingdom of the earth, but he is not your God." [226]

Eckhart'd have us pursue life without pursuit. *Santa's* dead but
Wear the suit? Even the Christ who suffered pains short shrift?

Moses's final assent to Yahweh's plan to torch the Cosmos?
"OK, OK. Ach JA—'blot me out **or** spare the living.'" Nobler

We'd have it read '**And** spare?' [Less distance from forgiving].
SUCH is the holy text that's quoted for the Meister's ENDS?

I'd look it up but trust his fusséd Faustian **pretense**. **For way**
Of life's promoted, in an **altered** fashion. NO image, impulse,

Gravitas, all life consigned to passion: salvation in non-being,
Stiff the mortal. Or pillage door and enter through the portal?

Suffering's *given credence*, measure, midway through his tome, a
Fleshly zest impressed on stolid affirmation, Let be or yessed.

FOUR

"'It is due to the fact that people esteem God so little. If people esteemed God as they should, it would be almost impossible for them ever to fall from grace.' And it is a good teaching that people should conduct themselves in this world just as if they were dead. Saint Gregory says: 'No one can possess God in such measure as one who is thoroughly dead to the world.'" [83]

The democrats would HAVE me just as it is, thoroughly dead,
If death is but a fever. Into my 7th wife and not deceive her? I

Beg to differ. This last an iffer. And speak yet from silk plush.
They have me currently in State. A last Big Mac is on my *gilded*

Plate. I see them with their clicking jowls procure a grimace. I
See the limit. All Hell is there. On gilded chair, from Nancy to

The Schumer. To *think* I defeated *even* Sleepy Joe! Had his mask
Peeled, elder, slow. Tremendous! Some 30 billions. Bigly was

The prize for sure. Even Obama rued his Fate, so chewed he
Humbled by a gilded slate. The teeth were right. I'll sleep this

Night I'll rest. But what's that tingle on my chest? A maggot?
A VP? Worm? a faggot? Dared me to brag it? Goooooonight!

FIVE

"In the same enjoyment in which God loves himself, he enjoys all things. With the same enjoyment with which God enjoys himself, he enjoys all creatures, not as creatures, but he enjoys the creatures as God. . . . I alone bring all creatures back to God. Look to see how all of you are doing!" [76]

"There are enthusiasms. People worship *D.J.T. turds,* automobiles
Cerebral Palsy, Fashion. Sniff Genitals and call it Affirmation,

Lift *cardboard Satans,* snipe at crowds, attend church, weddings,
Detonate airports, angle in polluted lakes, sleep, pursue altered

States of consciousness, circumstantial ethics. Laugh and weep
Seemingly in no odd season, step off buses, consult Plato and

Muktananda, Sakyamuni, Christ. Wash semen from their linen,
Cleanse their navels, insert suppositories, powder primp gargle,

Gag. Enter Taxis, restaurants, Galleries, silence, treaties. Make
Wills money love. Urinate, spit, sneeze sigh expire rot embrace,

Rattle smoke burn, control relinquish, predict, hope, discover,
Disclaim deny, deceive refute, strangle skewer, lacerate. Love."

SIX

"Thus soul that is to know God must be so established and fixed in God that nothing can make an impression on it—neither joy nor love nor sorrow nor anything else could take the soul from its own course. . . . Similarly the soul should be equally distant from all earthly matters so that it is not nearer to one than another." [139]

How very Zen! One hopes at even in one's dealings, even with
Despair. The urgency is There. Lift a leg and piss on your facile

Reality. Reminds us of the seer so *caught on* given koan that year
Her toddler strayed and drowned she was so *scant* disturbed she

Fixed on task impervious to son's distress and reached Satori!
Such deals of discipline or Ethics? The notion potion prevents

A consciousness of all ephemera: all equidistant nagging on the
Soul. For soul is solid! Sold? Small price the friend who alerted

To <u>friend's</u> despair cautioned indifference inhaled the local air,
Pissed in a jug. This self-control angling into void, devoid of a

Fellow-followed task then *sought* among all listings for the MD
Freed of *karmic* seeds *to treat his infernal* concupiscent *yearnings*.

SEVEN

"When the soul comes into the light of reason, then it knows nothing of opposition.
Whatever falls away from *this* kind of light falls down into mortality and dies. A
third result of the purity of the soul is that it is not inclined to anything. Whatever
is inclined toward another object dies and has no permanency." [86]

Light? By Jesu Christ it's dark in here. And the aroma? I only
Smell **myself?** No after-shave to sweeten scent, I'm **bent for**

Mighty rot. What is IS not. The Sanction's Universal. And 'D
Prefer some AC in this coffin. Was in the offing! Cheaply so.

Bilious. Furious. That VP tuned up for Pence. Come! Hence!
You're Potus now AND scantly opposition. My lower left the

Itching. Could wriggle in this state, be great! Just here or even
Deeper, more *mysterious*. Serious; were soon my time 'D come.

Father Son And Holy Ghost? *Quickest* suckling earn the most.
The chanter rancid. Am far past ant's id. But brain is active. A

Retroactive. *Tense cheek* the left to fire a fart. Now settle, clown.
Was POTUS itself yet lacking Crown, heel-spur further down.

EIGHT

"Indeed, even if the most extreme suffering were to occur and you were to feel some pain or suffering, it would still be completely turned around. For you would have to accept it as the best thing from God, since it must of necessity be the best way of all. This is because God's being requires him to wish what would be the best." [397-398]

Such odd compassion! And This is passion? Detachment from
The awful in *cheerful* vast assumption that it's awesome? Torrid

Horrid? Massive passive? We *squeeze* the grope despite the *grip?*
Which witch endures the fire? God's heavenly choir? Which **prior?**

'Tis discipline? Desire? A leverage on the higher? Surpasses *God*
OR Christ the Son. For Son endured a facile pain. So taken by

Indifference *faced* no loss. No *human* cost. To *happy* perch upon
God's loving Tree. And Meister Eckhart's worthy Dreckwort.

For any seeking judgment? The fashioning of Cosmos was His
Hedgement? From cheat to asp the widest gasp, to *human lapse*

PERHAPS? Jehovah WILLED this venture into birth. SUCH
Was the Genesis of Earth. Willful soulful ruddy-bloody Mirth.

NINE

"What God has given and what God promises to give—that is amazing, inconceivable, and unbelievable. And that is as it should be, for if it were comprehensible and believable things would not be right. God is in all things. . . . Everything God created six thousands ago—and even more—as he made the world, God creates now all at once. God is in everything. . . ." [65]

"Told me you were a pantheist. That's *right*. Couldn't remember
The term. God's everywhere, *Justin*. Got it from a book. Makes

Sense, doesn't it? In arschloch and gas burst bellies, in cancer &
Maggots, gangrene and *goat shit,* **scabies** and shingles, pustules

And Hydrogen bombs, Napalm and centipedes, Nerve gas and
Black widows. Everywhere. Simply *everywhere*. Keeps me going.

When I pull the scab off I say God's in there. In *some remote and*
Peculiar fashion *He's in there, Justin,* certain as syphilis. & when

We die, Justin. Know what happens then? We feed the plants.
It's a lovely belief, Justin. Helps me through *the night*. Leavens

My *afternoons*. Justin, don't turn away. Don't laugh. I **love** you.
We issued from the same genitals. See the holes in my hands?"

TEN

"So if you want to be this same Christ and God, empty yourself of everything which the eternal Word did not assume. The eternal Word did not assume a human being, so empty yourself of everything which is purely personal and peculiarly you and assume human nature purely, then you will be the same in the eternal Word as human nature is in him. . . . For if you are just, then everything which is in the Old and New Testaments will be fulfilled in you." [104]

Into a depression on the Emerald turf went 88 Buckets of the
Gilded rats' eyes. The shallow pond was ready for gelded DJT

Who belly flopped and *paddled* around in glee. Was not a sea.
Though fancied it an ocean. Charon **clapped** to pee and paid

A *wary weird devotion,* dipping fingers in to sample DT's lotion.
Was viscous, tart, imbued with tang, but **not** a potion. Was all

A soul had coveted since recent splinter to rebirth, was mirth
Beyond a shallow pond, was mighty penthouse in the greatest

Tower, bliss beyond **all** mortal power, a noble **it** of Holy juice,
And unencumbered by drain or sluice, one Godly Missal-lake

Few would mistake as inchoate or token. & farts were such as
No frail Potus could emit, was *dream,* mad *scheme, unseemly* Soaking!

ELEVEN

"Eckhart goes on and comments that, as great as creative imagination is with
its divine capacity for birthing images, nevertheless, even in being creative we
experience an insufficiency. . . . there are times for letting go even of our images.
Such times constitute the *via negative* and they allow the soul to be true to its deepest
self, which, like God, is both nameless and eternally youthful." [Fox,185]

Likely the *least* literal excuse for ignoring the **Sistine Chapel?**
For Pillaging the **David?** For silencing **Hammerklavier?** FOR

A stillborn **Shaksper?** The deceitful torment and perseverance
Of the trip to **Starry Night?** For a billion-fold presumption of

Wretched struggle and release toward **All** that man endured to
Engender **human trans**cendence? Is there truly so little in the

Child's first scrawl, no dignity in self-expression? This 13th era
Master who would will a 13 hour trip *on crystal meth toward some*

Universal sovereignty that effaces every partial? We've **known**
The martial, what *terror of human toil* exists *in U.S. atomic fusion.*

Our Einsteins will to us **their** sullen wisdom. Yet Eckhart is
Trance past even *chance or* psychic solution. *Efface the* **planet?**

TWELVE

"Nothing so much hinders the soul's understanding of God as time and space.
Time and space are parts of the whole but God is one. So if the soul is to recognize
God, it must do so beyond time and space. For God is neither this nor that in the
way of the manifold things of earth. . . . so long as the soul is conscious of time or
space or any other earthly representation, it cannot know God." [139-140]

One even fears a **forced** detachment. Love the sky? The **earth?**
Love wife love pet? Love *one above* another? Martin **Buber** flees

In terror. This cherry-picker having seen *God's utter* once? Nay 3
Times peril-differ? And where the **error?** To worship OTHER?

And Meister homing timeless in divinity. Would lapse in honey?
God bless the weak or partial? Forgive the martial? Collapse at

Gaps, forswear the torn? Forsake the riven? Endure but Shun a
Given? I find the promise Godlike? oddly human. Far from that

Surge to kneel or genuflect, the corpse of Christ securely on my
Back, yes God Himself enduring self, would toast fine wine or

Ordinaire to health and riches. *As far as such as* Trump or certain
Groundlings place beneath the bitches' *pastor,* disappoint the Meister.

THIRTEEN

"Now Jesus says: 'Young man, I tell you to get up!'. . . What now is God's 'declaration'? It is God's *deed,* and this deed is so noble and elevated that God *alone* accomplishes it. Know then that all our perfection and all our bliss depend on the fact that the individual goes through and beyond all creation and all temporality and all being, and enters the foundation that is without foundation." [128]

> This *death-box* is so dark I can *rely on* my own thoughts. *And if*
> There IS a wench *I* can't discern it. Some massage **message**
>
> Must Intern it. *A silence?* Impeachment? So *mangled* brain had
> Angled what a peach meant? If Giuliani (sic?) thought *that was*
>
> Piani then **it** was grand indeed; misread or read, we stumbled
> At the steed [*which shoe* to polish?]. This Fate is foolish! Trapt
>
> Here like a gopher. A Deal without an offer. Could likely rent
> The plush, the laugh, a lover's seat per Haps. And *this* the final
>
> Curtain? To choke in my own gas! And belch and piss? THIS
> Merman. Scarcely white! If knew the time I'd sleep the *frigging*
>
> Night. No tweets no trill. The odor *makes me* ill. *And **This** the*
> Time to take my pill? Half an Aspirin? Make an **ASS yearn!**

FOURTEEN

"Unity is a negation of negation. All creatures carry a negation within themselves; one denies that it is another. . . . One angel denies that it is another. But God has the negation of negation; he is one and denies every other, for outside God there is nothing. . . . when I deny God something, I understand something of him, namely, what he is not. Now even this must be done away with. God is one. He is the negation of negation." [190]

Am I indeed the spokesman for the partial? Do I cling *to* broad
Nostalgia for the incomplete? Is there lure to insufficient? For

The lack of even **lack** assures salvation? This God our Meister
Slips beneath the lens seems wicked, even nightmare. And dare

I submit and let alone examine? Can Yahweh sport no Face nor
Harbor visage? The early settlers in their cave were prompted a

Submission to *odd* image, and yet were tens of thousands years
Proactive even before God's **title itself** was savage. What holy

Name *assigned* to Deity devoid of texture, "Nada, nichts"? One
Kneels to ghost-less substance. One kneels? What Omni-none

Existent mercy quite effaced? "Suffer little children come unto
Me?" And **this** from 33 AD? Take pierced ye **take** the **Christ!**

FIFTEEN

"It is good that a person has a peaceful life; it is better that a person bear a troublesome life with patience. But best of all is that a person can have peace even in the very midst of trouble. . . . If the situation is such that he can better perceive God when he is in peaceful circumstances where he is comfortable, this is due to his own insufficiency and not to anything on God's part. For God is equally in all things. . . . The one who knows God best is the one who recognizes him equally everywhere." [138-139]

Solipsism minus self? The Meister leaving mule beside a weary
Mountain, scales the better, willing fetter *just* exist. Such is HIS

Faith, even stage *4 cancer* fiction with the proper lack of stance,
A bitless servile **mad** detachment. The Peak exists **mind's eye**

In non-existence, for God if **all** is absence, *pain at* best a nuisance.
Once is pled in *thought and deed, odd* bliss itself. A source? Were

On the shelf a *quest* a symptom. Eckhart is discipline forsaking
Effort; a *billion forks* in mortal road yield *firm* direction. *Brute soil*

Is tilled; the view is *blossom*. For fruit is *handsome*. Even *the bitter*
Fitter. Ease bow *across* the strings, *reward* all things, the sounds

Are silence? God's will *cannot exist, a* bounteous twist, an even
Folly-holy. Such *is* the wholly, incontinence our **mental** Foley.

SIXTEEN

"Whoever knows God knows that all creatures are nothing. . . . when anything is
placed over against God, then it is nothing. . . . the soul wanting to perceive God
must forget itself and lose itself. For if it perceives itself, then it does not perceive
God. But in God the soul finds itself again. . . . In the degree to which the soul has
separated itself from itself and from all things, to the same degree the soul knows
itself fully." [140]

The pond of rats' eyes morphs into a vivid churning spiral, an
Angry swirl sucking the DT under, while Assorted Creatures

Rasp from the very edge a horrific mélange: odd sanction and
Approval. The DJT flails limbs about, cutting ill swaths amid

The Bubbling stink. Is 45th full sucked, a fearsome flotsam on
The heady brew? The suck is You! Corporeal slush reduced at

Last to fervid shake, no pity for the Fret and hunger, 45th, his
Mortal danger, inhaling copious draughts of rats' eyes *shedding*

Gilt and guilt, a vortex surging deeply 45th. DJT cries out for a
Piteous grip, a tong, a claw, to think a demon 'D *temper* strait,

Find *mortal fellow* in the pitted, sucking rat-*encrusted fright* [was
It *Moor-born* hate, urge a dirge, vindictive, cosmic anchor**ite?**].

SEVENTEEN

"For if you love God as he is God or mind or person or picture, all that must be
dropped. How then shall you love him? You should love him as he is, a not-God,
not-mind, not-person, not image—even more as he is a pure, clear One, separate
from all twoness. And we should sink eternally from something to nothing into
this One. May God help us to do this. Amen." [180]

Prayer to a vacant predication? Mater *Theresa'd* vent frustration
With her calloused *hands*. Such *are her Meister's* harsh demands?

The rosary the crucifix? The image sticks. We're caught in not?
In ought? He'd sink all worship to a holy phantom? How else

This fountain? A summon from a vortex into Void? Anciently
Deployed in hopes of water? Divinity's *stern* Mother? *All other?*

Which of us endure Our Father? *Bother?* Which of us the Son?
Anyone? *There* on an arid crest the brooding Christ, there Ice?

There Wily Graham? There I AM. There Iamb? Even our bold
Anapest is lonely. Dactyl sinketh toward decay. Trochees burn

A poet's skull. The metaphor is ugly, cruel. Pity the 23rd Psalm
Or *bard* that wrote it. The need to quote it. All soul demote it?

EIGHTEEN

"The master says: Heaven cannot receive any strange impression. No painful need
that would seek to bring heaven out of its course can have any effect. Thus the soul
that is to know God must be so established and fixed in God that nothing can make

an impression on it—neither joy nor suffering nor love nor sorrow nor anything else could take the soul from its own course. Heaven in all places is equally distant from the earth." [139]

Our God Jehovah that ignited Adam, Eve, to life was blandly
Secular as a corporate merger, a mortgage broker; sadly stolid

As a Potus fence, dividing pair to each his given share, fusséd
Lair to prune at early AM, small hint of coming *mayhem* in the

Ride, all pride denied of blessing, rancor. Such was the anchor
Our primeval fate, such comfort-*able* trait, a judge well-coiffed

And tall *but not to fault;* for chosen stylist had an eye for fashion
Envy any Eve, no wayward pledge in his Fraternity, no hanker

Either love, disdain, plainest heritage and trim, yet regally thin,
Remote from carnal appetite, and in **his cups forthright** and

Gladsome, unlike that Lucifer of late [imbued with narcissistic
Mate]; seems SO unfair *Creation* bled its dew upon **their** plate.

NINETEEN

"But when a person is too hot, he or she has no comfort in clothing. That is exactly the way it is with all creatures. For this reason, it is true that all creatures bear bitterness within themselves. On the other hand, it is quite true that all creatures bear within themselves a form of consolation, like skimmed honey. All the good that can exist in creatures—all their honey—is gathered together in God." [152]

What wretched boil of clams BE itching through my innards?
This stomach's kick't for soccer. What evil do I succor? What

Curdle eats upon my groin? Is like an inner girdle. I belch the
Awful Mess. Saliva's sweet. 10,000 Big Macs take and eat, I'm

Honey for the **homing.** So dark! I'd light the lot. The **ordure**
Odor. **The stink.** And so much time to think! Obscene their

Theme. To **tweet** the hideous lot! A wad of corrugated snot a
Hunger. *This* mass erupts my chest. Boils leak my lack. I'd itch

The fact. And wherefore the spill from every crack? **Alack** it's
Crack attack. These scavengers upon the sacral. My mackerel!

The **fact** will? Oft willed self-image to a permanent setting. Is
Heard what I'm regretting? The torment? This pus a torrent!

TWENTY

"I speak of spiritual satisfaction when the highest peak of the soul is not so humbled
that it drowns in a feeling of pleasure but rather stands in might above it. For people
are in a state of spiritual satisfaction only when love and sorrow of creatures cannot
humble the highest peak of their souls. I call a creature whatever we perceive and
see beneath God." [479]

Most strange! Deranged? And yet his textual pronouncement.
We run in horror? Or simply terror. This strange assertion of

The Meister's touted firm detachment! The message logged in
Fogged *translation?* Or certified Creation? To speak of peak as

Spiritual condition, a Royal state approaches what was served
Upon one's Regal plate? Asséssed spirit? Fear it. *No* secretive

Insertion in a blameless *quest* when elsewhere the Biblical text
Is similarly expressed. What royalty accrues to fancifully legal

Elevation? No toiling class, no perspiration needed, our loft a
Loft, nobility is seeded. When each athwart a chariot Eckhart

Dances to the Kingdom, microseconds wrenched to rapture!
Such chapter? Odd elegance, the chosen prance their captor.

TWENTY-ONE

"For all are our brothers and not just those who are related to by family, nation, race, or religion. We all share divine origins, a noble heritage of such great dignity. He subscribes to the universalist doctrine of salvation, that God wills all persons to be saved." [Fox,308]

Largess as such to grace the common touch, my quarrel were
Not with brotherhood or such salvation; but that Fox repeats

No sentiment we find in Eckhart-sermon. Nobility I'd *grant* a.
Spot in Paradise at least to any vermin-hood had ceased from

Venal pursuit, nay silk or ermine. What leverage is there to id
Man Purim? The textual evidence is lacking. Adhere to Nada

In either being or becoming? Am glad my air conditioner is
Humming. And not-God in his nothing lacks the voucher *or*

Credentials. The Meister guards *a universal* Void, nor *fashioned*
Or destroyed, nor given, or employed, an attitude at best, a

Fiction. Again I must rely on diction. The path to rendering
Any modern tongue *were* rocky. With motley often mockery?

TWENTY-TWO

"Yes, the humble need not beg God so much as bid him, for the heights of divinity can disregard everything else but the depths of humility, for the humble person and God are one and not two. Such humble people are powerful with God because they are so powerful with themselves. . . . Yes, by God, if such a person were in hell, God would be constrained to join that person there, and hell itself would be for such a person like heaven." [167]

Even bones attacked and fevered. And brain is viscous. I'm
Peeing through my sockets. For I lowered the Interest *Rate to*

Eye the rocket? Even the GOP hadn't sought it [our fearless
Folks a-aped as liberal economics] or jokes? [a demographic

Prattle]. I sliced that sacerdotal Cohen. *Sitting squat* just where
He rots, suckling *the lower teat,* that snivel, that limp-*kneed devil.*

Eat this! You weevil! Imbibe **my** hide it's snug in goo, a paste
A spew, and **one remaining** shoe. Even ITS tug **against my**

Spur? This *casket is no bore.* I'm angling for *God's oath* or more,
I'm screaming. Even my rancid pupils rest upon the temples

Interbred with hair. Is votive. GRIM devotion is **my** motive.
Killing *time?* Betrothed to fetal-futile ache, to chance, design.

2019

SOURCES
D.A.Vid

David Swartz

Copyright owners

Page vii print--owned by Stephanie Swartz Janat
Makan, daughter, her photograph
of her parents, possessed by D. Swartz, myself.
Page xii print---owned by Tara Janat Makan,
granddaughter, taken by her at her 17th year,
possessed by D. Swartz, myself.
Page xiv print--owned by D. Swartz, myself, taken
of me by my wife, J.E. Swartz,1982.
Page xv Print--owned by M Hassan, taken by M, Hassan, friend of my
daughter, of Mona Janat Makan, granddaughter, at 18.
Page xvi print--snapshot owned by M. Albahary, taken by Stephanie Swartz,
my daughter, of M. Albahary, his 60th birthday.
Page 45 print--owned by D. Swartz, myself, ink drawing by me,1968.
Page 59 Print--owned by Tara Janat Makan, my
granddaughter, her ink drawing, 2016.
Page 69 print--snapshot by myself and wife, owned by wife, J. E, Swartz, 2019.
Page 103 print--front page clipping, Des Moines Register. 1970, copyright owner
unknown, in my possession.
Page 121 print—owned by J.E. Swartz. Stephanie, daughter, with poet, myself.
Front cover print--picture owned by M. Albahary, of David Swartz, myself, this
May 2020, in my possession.

David Swartz has permission to use all these prints
but page 91, the owner or individual depicted likely deceased.

123

Printed in the United States
By Bookmasters